OBJECTIONS TO ROMAN CATHOLICISM

All the contributors to this volume are Roman Catholics.

It has been the intention of the contributors to the two previous volumes, OBJECTIONS TO CHRISTIAN BELIEF and OBJECTIONS TO HUMANISM, to acknowledge openly the difficulties they encounter in the faith which they themselves hold.

Until very recently the image of the Roman Catholic Church has been—and in many respects continues to be—one of such unassailable authority that few outside this Church would have supposed that it was possible for committed Roman Catholics to acknowledge, let alone publicly to utter, difficulties they came up against in their faith.

The publication of this book is thus historic in two ways. It demonstrates the radical change which has been coming in the public image of the Roman Catholic Church since the initiative of Pope John XXIII. And, perhaps of more enduring importance, it is witness to the rise of an informed and courageous laity, whose faith is of a strength and seriousness to feel the need of further and deeper discussion about the implications of Roman Catholicism—and this particularly in the light of the rapidly changing world of today.

This is a book of great moment. Archbishop Roberts' challenging contribution on contraception will be of particular and personal importance to Roman Catholics. But this book will be read with enjoyment by thinking people of *all* persuasions and should provide excellent material for discussion groups.

Uniform with this volume

OBJECTIONS TO CHRISTIAN BELIEF
OBJECTIONS TO HUMANISM

OBJECTIONS TO ROMAN CATHOLICISM

Magdalen Goffin
John M. Todd
Frank Roberts
Professor H. P. R. Finberg
Rosemary Haughton
G. F. Pollard
Archbishop Thomas Roberts, S.J.

*Edited with an Introduction by
Michael de la Bedoyere*

CONSTABLE · LONDON

Published by Constable & Co. Ltd.
10–12 Orange Street
London, W.C.2

© 1964 Constable & Co. Ltd.

First published 1964

ERRATA

8 line 34	For Schmedt read Smedt
96 line 10	For the powerful thinkers read these powerful thinkers
98 line 24	For has been read had been
101 line 13	For antecedency read antecedents
103 line 11	For a French Dominican read the French Dominican
108 line 5	For Leo XIII read Leo XII
153 footnote 1	For *Op. cit.* read *From Glory to Glory,* Texts from the Mystical Writings of Gregory of Nyssa, selected and with an Introduction by Jean Daniélou, S.J. Translated and edited by Herbert Musurillo, S.J. John Murray 1963.

MADE AND PRINTED IN GREAT BRITAIN BY
THE GARDEN CITY PRESS LIMITED
LETCHWORTH, HERTFORDSHIRE

CONTENTS

Introduction

MICHAEL DE LA BEDOYERE

'*OBJECTIONS to Roman Catholicism*' could never have been written but for Pope John's 'aggiornamento' or bringing up to date of the Roman Catholic Church. (Having twice already used the term 'Roman', I propose to drop it in the rest of this introduction. I do this, of course, not with any intention of offending other Communions who object to the Church in Communion with the See of Peter calling itself 'Catholic' *tout court*, but simply for convenience.)

The more we think of Pope John, the more remarkable —indeed unique—he seems. Here was an old man who made no claims whatever to any special learning or unusual experience. His career, as a priest and Roman diplomat, was not exceptional—except perhaps for his keen sense of humour and his love of telling good stories. I like particularly the story of Pope John, when Nuncio in Paris, asking why it was that when a too daringly *décolletée* lady appeared at a reception, no one looked at the lady but all eyes turned to him? It was perhaps such stories which caused the more serious French clerics to frown at the Nuncio's ways and to feel certain that whoever might succeed Pope Pius XII, at least they would be spared the simple-minded and tactless Cardinal Roncalli, as he then was.

But the intelligent French turned out, as they often do, to be completely wrong. Cardinal Roncalli became Pope John—Pope John who changed the face of Catholic history.

In my view, there is only one explanation of this utterly unexpected outcome. It is simply that Pope John possessed the virtues that tend to be rare in the higher ranks of the Catholic clergy. These, bound down by a deep sense of responsibility and the 'image' of the essentially unchanging Church, founded by Christ and enduring, against all human probabilities, for nineteen hundred years and more, always looked backwards. Their sense of spiritual and historical destiny blinded them, to a considerable extent at least, to the two vital factors of true religion: Our Lord on the one hand and you and me whom Our Lord evangelized and died for. The clerical machine took over. Naturally, I am writing in gross generalizations. The great army of saints and holy people through the centuries witnessed in their lives to all that is implied in the love of God. The great spiritual and mystical men and women lived close to God, retaining their Catholic orthodoxy and loyalty. But the Church, as such, from early Christianity and the age of the martyrs, moved on, in the words of Bishop De Schmedt, to 'triumphalism, clericalism and juridicism'. Let me say at once, in case I am misunderstood, that this triumphalism, clericalism and juridicism is perfectly consistent in practice with holy and spiritually devoted private lives from popes and bishops down to the simplest and least educated of Catholics. But the policies and outlook of the Church itself at the level of popes, bishops and clergy have, in my view, often removed them very far indeed from the imitation of Christ.

To get back, then, to Pope John. This peasant, un-learned, homely, fat figure of a pope instinctively did things which popes had not done for centuries, if ever. In the grandeur and pomp of his great position he remained an ordinary man following (one could say courageously, except that he probably never thought in such terms) his natural, almost untutored spiritual and commonsense instincts. He lived very close to Our Lord, humbly and unassumingly. And the most extraordinary thing he did was the utterly irresponsible gesture of one day saying, in effect, 'Let's have an Ecumenical Council'! By doing so, he changed the course of Catholic history.

To Pope John's miraculous irresponsibility there came an almost equal 'irresponsibility' on the part of large numbers of Catholics. Suddenly fresh air seemed to blow through the Church. Bishops, priests, nuns, lay-folk felt the wind of a new freedom. They could think for themselves. Instead of signing on the intricate mass of dotted lines deriving in ever greater numbers from the Counter-Reformation and the ever-increasing authoritarianism, both in religion and politics, of modern times, so many of us became human beings within the religious context. I underline this, because it is quite absurd to suppose, as some conservative religious authorities do suppose, that Catholics are going to lose their faith, just because they now feel the right to think for themselves. Take the example of the primacy of conscience which Cardinal Bea has so strongly defended. This is, of course, an essential teaching of the Catholic Church. But its practical interpretation in the past has been that a true conscience is a conscience that accepts the teaching of the Church—and, if in doubt, blindly. But a true conscience must accept, however deplorably in the eyes of some Churchmen, whatever one seriously and thoughtfully believes to be right and true. Not to do so would be gravely wrong, and it is God, not the Church, who alone can finally judge the sincerity of the choices that a man makes.

It would, of course, be utterly wrong on my part to suggest that Pope John in creating this religious wind of change had the remotest intention of starting a kind of spiritual free-for-all. On the contrary, his instinctive call for a second Vatican Council was to bring the Church up-to-date through the labours of those best-equipped and with the most weight—the bishops and their theological advisers. One recalls that this massive effort was originally to be secret, both as regards the workers in the Council and the non-Catholic observers. But in our times this soon proved to be impossible. The consequence was, of course, that the whole world became the Council's audience and everyone was in a position to study, think about, and discuss the views of the Fathers of the Council. This inevitably meant that religiously alive people, Catholics and other Christians, felt a fresh surge of freedom with the right to think and discuss for oneself the relevance and quality of Catholic teaching today. The number, capable of and interested in using this freedom, is to this day probably very small indeed. The mass of Catholics, I should think, are still hardly aware of any change, except for certain liturgical alterations of a still very minor nature—changes which are, for the most part, unpopular at any rate in English-speaking countries. But there exists a minority of

Catholic clergy and laity (steadily growing, I believe) who fully realize that Pope John set in motion what will prove to be an unprecedented Catholic reform. As intelligent, fervent and interested Catholics they cannot be prevented from studying and discussing with a strong, fresh sense of freedom the means of rejuvenating the ancient Church and bringing it into tune with the values, spiritual and temporal, of the latter part of the twentieth-century. And it is this 'new look' from the past to the present which, I take it, is the most important change, stemming straight from Pope John's saintliness, humanity and commonsense.

All this remains far from being to the taste of (probably) the overwhelming number of Catholics today. And it is particularly resented by great numbers in the English-speaking countries and (I suppose) in backward parts of Europe, by no means excluding Italy, the country of the Holy Office (with an inquisitor in every country) which feels itself to have the special office of maintaining a fully authoritarian Church. There seems to be a deadly fear that any suggestion of Catholics really thinking for themselves must cause early shipwreck to the barque of Peter. This view hardly flatters the bishops, priests and teachers, most of whom take it for granted that the Catholic masses are incapable of more than a simple rustic piety, totally unrelated to the world in which they live. It is a far cry from the enthusiasm of early Christianity.

One recognizes, of course, that reforms and changes cannot be precipitated; but this is no excuse for virtually doing nothing in a safety-first atmosphere—an atmosphere which is, I think, already causing, in part at least, a steadily increasing 'leakage' from the Church through modern communications which bring to every citizen a standard of values remote indeed from the Christian tradition. Despite the fears of the conservative bishops, it seems obvious that in the years to come the fully-educated, free, enlightened Catholic will prove to be the one best able to cope with this increasing danger. And this brings me to my main task—introducing *Objections to Roman Catholicism*.

The writers of these essays are all writing in the spirit of Pope John. They are of the minority who fully realize that it is impossible today to face up to the great questions and problems of Christianity without being free to say what they really think and believe. This may involve certain risks from the point of view of theologically-trained bishops and priests. But if the Catholic Church of the future is to face constructively the growing religious and spiritual laxity, not only of so many baptized Christians but even of Catholics religiously trained in terms of the quite different conditions of the past, it can only be in an atmosphere of freedom and *personal* integrity and honesty.

These 'Objections' then are objections to the outdated traditions and the historical weaknesses which, despite the reform initiated by Pope John, persist. Evidently, it will take many years to carry out a reform of this magnitude and difficulty. Even so, the wind of change is blowing already with far greater force than anyone a few years ago could dream. The writers of the seven essays are all laymen and laywomen, with the notable exception of Archbishop Roberts. To have attempted to produce this book with the Catholic *imprimatur* would, of course, have been absurd. Its whole point is to break new ground in the spirit of Pope John. Apart from suggesting the subjects I have in no way altered the essays except for a number of 'cuts' due solely to space considerations. I believe they will be of great interest to all concerned with Christianity today and I hope they will become the subject of widespread discussion, that the truth in them may be cherished and any weaknesses overlooked.

May I end on one note—a note to which I have not so far referred. Perhaps the most enduring and most important 'change of mind' we owe to Pope John is Christian Unity. I have lived my Catholic life as a journalist and writer in terms of disunity. By that I mean that I have lived in terms of an ideal of unity which simply meant that unity was just another word for submission to the Roman Catholic Church. It was a form of proselytism. This was never to my taste, and I should like to pay a tribute to the late Cardinal Hinsley who at least realized that there were many forms of practical unity (for example, in personal relations and moral and civic matters) which could draw Christians of different persuasions together. But the next two Cardinals of Westminster hardly followed his lead, and today we look, in very different terms indeed, to Pope John and Cardinal Bea for the closing of the Christian ranks in the face of mounting secularism and, too often, a God-lessness which, if not indoctrinated as in Communist countries, increasingly permeates Western Society.

I recently read a most interesting article by the missionary Archbishop of Mwanza, Mgr. Blomjous. He suggested that perhaps it was not God's will that all Christians should unite and become one Church. 'It seems', he wrote, 'that religious pluralism is part of God's plan. Can we yet affirm that the Lord sent His Church into the world to reunite all men in the unity of the same faith? We are bound to face this grave question: what is the theological significance of religious pluralism? What does God want to say to us in the midst of the multiplicity of religions . . . ? It looks as though Christian divisions will last until the end of time. We must ask ourselves the question: what is God trying to say to us in the light of these divisions?'

However this be, there can be no doubt that the writers of these essays are creating a Catholic 'image' which will powerfully help mutual *understanding* between a 'free', but essentially orthodox, Roman Catholicism and the views and traditions of other Communions to—as I believe—the Greater Glory of God.

And finally let me insist that each writer has been left entirely free to speak his or her own mind, whether orthodox or unorthodox. It is for the reader to consider and study each article, approving or disapproving, but at least doing so with the realisation that the world of tomorrow will not be the same as the world of yesterday. In its essential spiritual and moral teaching the Church of Rome cannot change; but it can and has developed by deepening its understanding of divine revelation and pruning the rank growths which have flourished through human credulity and sentimentality. In the past these were acceptable; but I doubt whether they will remain so in the future. We Catholics have to prepare for a religiously sterner and more contemporary twenty-first century.

MICHAEL DE LA BEDOYERE
EDENBRIDGE
JULY 1964

Some Reflexions on Superstition and Credulity

MAGDALEN GOFFIN

SOME time in what was to prove to be the last summer of his life Dr Johnson paid a visit to his old college at Oxford. There it was remarked that a certain Mr Chamberlayne had given up great prospects in the Church of England to become a Roman Catholic. Boswell, who had his own reasons for probing this particular subject, reports the conversation in some detail. In the course of giving his approbation to this exercise of an erroneous conscience Johnson made the well known observation that 'a good man of timorous disposition and in great doubt of his acceptance with God, and pretty credulous might be glad of a Church where there are so many helps to heaven. I would be a Papist if I could. I have fear enough, but an obstinate rationality prevents me.'

Roughly fifty years later sentiments of a similar kind were expressed by a very different man in a very different

15

manner. The overwrought Newman was to write at Palermo, 'Oh that thy creed were sound! For thou dost soothe the heart, thou Church of Rome', saying in verse something of what from the Eternal City itself, he had written home to a friend, '. . . what mingled feelings come upon one . . . in the place of martyrdom and burial of Apostles and saints; . . . in the city to which England owes the blessing of the Gospel. But then, on the other hand, the superstitions, or rather what is far worse, the solemn reception of them as part of Christianity. But then, again, the extreme beauty and costliness of the churches; and then, on the contrary, the knowledge that the most famous of them was built (in part) by indulgences. Really this is a cruel place.'

To Johnson, ill, old, and saddened by the certainty of dying, Rome had one kind of attraction. To Newman, seeking the kind of authority which Anglicanism by its very nature was unable to give, it had another. Even Macaulay could respond to her antiquity and staying power in a celebrated passage of rhetoric, while what with the *Lives of the Saints* and opening and shutting doors in the face of agitated Archdeacons, the young J. A. Froude himself fell victim to a mild attack of Roman fever. But the inoculation took. Thereafter he was to spend the rest of his life paying more attention to the Queen of England than the Queen of Heaven, and it was not until towards the end of it that he wrote in his journal, 'Yet the Roman Church after all is something . . . It will survive all other forms of Christianity, and without Christianity what is to become of us? . . . The philosophers and writers have done for Protestantism as a positive, manly, and intellectually credible explanation of the world. The old organism and the old superstition steps into its ancient dominion finding it swept and garnished.'

This last prophecy, for a number of reasons, must now be seen to be very wide of the mark, yet the fact remains that for an educated Western Christian, historically, logically, and aesthetically, the claims of Rome are very strong indeed. Why then these mingled feelings? Why is it that her power to repel is as strong as her power to attract, that the call of antiquity, the claims of logic, all the seductions provided by a beautiful liturgy, frequently beckon in vain, and that hearts and minds, remain, not indifferent indeed, but hostile? The answer given, expressed in one way or another, amounts to this: we cannot love you, we cannot join you, because let your credentials be ever so persuasive, your helps to heaven ever so numerous, your liturgy ever so splendid, in practice you invite us to worship but a shrunken god.

This is the meaning of superstition. It is, basically, any belief or practice inspired by an unworthy view of God. Although frequently they exist together, it is not to be confused with credulity which is an uncritical, ill-founded belief in supposed occurrences which are in fact contrary to known truth at any given time. To believe in eternal torment is superstitious, to believe that the holy house in Nazareth flew to Italy with all its furnishings is credulous.

When the Greeks considered that behaviour towards the Divine which was worthy of a human being they distinguished between *deisidaimonia* and *threskeia*, the one indicating an attitude determined by fear, the other too great a concentration on the religious rites themselves. Both *deisidaimon* and *threskos* were used to describe a superstitious man. The Christian emphasis is on what is worthy of God. The seventeenth century Platonist John Smith defines superstition as 'such an apprehension of God in the thoughts of men as renders Him grievous and burdensome to them, and so destroys all free and cheerful converse with Him; begetting in the stead thereof a forced and jejeune devotion void of inward life and love.'[1] For him superstition is a mixture of fear and flattery, its true cause a false opinion of a god made after the similitude of men, a god dreadful and terrible, gratified by slavish crouchings.

Both superstition and credulity are, in their application, relative terms. It would be grossly unfair and unhistorical to blame Abraham because he thought God could be propitiated by human sacrifice, or Pascal because he believed in the authenticity of the relic of the Crown of Thorns. These things are culpable only, in the case of superstition, when the progressive revelation of God among the few has so leavened the whole that to cling to unworthy notions about him is to sin against the light; in the case of credulity when the wider dissemination of knowledge has made reasonable assent to a certain occurrence impossible. It is hard to say if Justinian should be censured for considering homosexuality to be the cause of earthquakes, but Anselm of Canterbury should have known better than to have attributed spiteful behaviour to SS. Agnes and Lawrence because their church was deprived of its garden; and while much must be forgiven a convert it was distinctly credulous of the later Newman to believe the Holy Manger was preserved in Rome, and astonishing to learn that Cardinal Manning is said to have thought *incubi* and *succubae* really existed.

Unworthy ideas of God result in unworthy forms of worship. This flattery takes many shapes, but the fear which prompts it is three-fold. Fear of punishment in

[1] *Select Discourses. Of Superstition.* First edition, 1660. In this discourse we see that his respect for the Gospel makes Smith attempt to justify hell and the contemplation of it in contradiction to his own excellent principles.

another state; then, most persistently, fear which has its roots in ignorance and which attempts to use God as a means of controlling an imperfectly understood environment; finally fear that the evil doer will be struck down here and now. This last superstition was common to all Christians, from the New Testament story of Ananias and Sapphira to the popular nineteenth century evangelical tales about clergymen who dropped down dead while playing cards.

As Johnson himself well knew, the fundamental objections to Roman Catholicism are objections to Christian orthodoxy. His obstinate rationality prevented him from believing only those doctrines which Rome held in isolation from the rest of western Christendom, his scepticism extended only to peripheral matters considered by other Christians to be neither true nor needful. That this then is not an essay on the superfluous is due to the fact that despite their obvious external differences, shared attitudes of mind and convictions make the eighteenth century Protestant in a real sense closer to the modern Roman Catholic than is his descendant. For it is Rome's very conservatism and fidelity to Christian orthodoxy, her determination to hold on at any cost to doctrines which form part of the original belief and practice of Christians that so often lays her open to the charges which have accumulated against her.

The history of religion is the story of man's efforts to purify and deepen his understanding of God, to separate the accidents which necessarily modify and clothe the expression of a religion existing in historical time from the essential, universal experience of Supreme Being. Sometimes, when Rome gives an example of stunted growth in this respect, it is because her fidelity to revelation as all Christians once supposed it to be, together

19

with her instinct to preserve each item in the Creeds lest the whole should be dissolved, has proved stronger than her own and other people's insights into the nature of God. In considering her attitude towards the doctrine of hell this dilemma is seen at its sharpest.

J. S. Mill justly remarked that compared with the doctrine of endless torment any other objection to Christianity sinks into insignificance. In the past all Christians believed in hell on principle and enjoyed describing it in terms as grisly and crude as those employed by many Roman Catholics today. When enough people realized that, whatever the fate of those who repudiate God, a doctrine which implies that the Creator is less good than the creature must be false, then that doctrine had to be abandoned. Not without hesitations and quibbles, however, for the price of the abandonment was heavy. Rome is not yet prepared to pay it. Faithful to her view of revelation, she constantly and consistently preaches what she has received. In whatever imagery it is clothed, the existence of hell is still taught as part of the Faith without accepting which no Catholic can see God—a god whom if he believed what he was told, no one in his senses would wish to see. Nor, apart from some pitiful efforts here and there to minimize the number of the lost, has she tried to dilute its significance. Dr Arendzen, in *The Teaching of the Catholic Church* (1952), tells his readers, 'If all that was ever written, or painted, or carved expressive of the tortures of hell could be brought before us at a glance, it would certainly fall immeasurably short of the truth.' A book published in 1964 with the Southwark imprimatur and intended for Roman Catholic children in grammar schools, speaks of the physical fires of hell and the wicked writhing in envy and remorse for all eternity. Here credulity and superstition are combined.

We should, however, appreciate both the far-reaching implications of any rejection of orthodoxy, and admire the staunchness with which Rome has insisted on the annihilating effect of sin. Further, we must frankly face the fact that parodoxically those from all creeds most conscious of the love of God are frequently the very people who have held firmly to the doctrine of everlasting suffering. The explanation must surely be that it is a perversion of a truth, the truth, to use Von Hügel's term, of final consequences. Men can and do lose God by unrepentant rejection of him as he speaks with the voice of conscience. It is precisely because these great lovers of God saw the dreadfulness of this self-chosen negation and loss so clearly, that making use of current imaginative and conceptual expressions, they perverted it into an everlasting state of positive suffering. Since however the most morally sensitive today rightly revolt against this perversion, Catholic theologians who obstinately hold on to it are opposing the light and fostering a hideous superstition.

It was 'Purgatory Pick-Purse' rather than the actual idea of an intermediate state which really infuriated the sixteenth century reformers, but they came in time to think of the whole doctrine as 'foolishly invented and repugnant to the Word of God'. This was a pity, because however hard it is to believe that human beings are immortal, there is nothing either superstitious or credulous in the notion that, if they are, at death the majority of souls are too self-centred to be yet capable of being filled with the life of God himself. If we accept the Communion of Saints as a living reality, understand that every man is indeed a piece of the human continent, it is difficult to see that it is superstitious to pray for the dead, and even in some way, to share their suffering. The truth of religion is tested in man's experience. Many

Protestants have wished to pray for their dead, but have felt inhibited from doing so. Johnson's private diary records that on Easter Day he recommended his parents and his wife in prayer, but 'I did it only once, so far as might be lawful for me'. Luckily in modern times the Church of England cares more for valid religious experience than it does for an outmoded theology.

Unfortunately, what starts as a reasonable opinion may end in nonsensical certainty. An idea expressed simply is a very different thing from the same idea encrusted, elaborated, and drawn out with nightmare logic. A great many Roman Catholic beliefs and practices concerning purgatory are nothing more than, to quote Professor Leavis in an entirely different connexion, 'fossilized opinions masquerading as facts'. Worse, they are superstitious, for they encourage mechanical ideas about salvation and present for our worship 'a grievous and burdensome God, easy to be appeased by jejeune devotion devoid of inward life and love'.

Despite the austerity and dignity of the reference to purgatory in the Roman Mass, its pains are popularly understood to be similar to those of hell, the difference being that they will have an end. These sufferings are considered to be either strictly purgatorial, or satisfactional, that is the soul is expiating the sins of its earthly life. Some theologians hold one view, some another, some both. If seen with the eye of the spirit something of this may be meaningful, but unfortunately it is often stated in such a way as to suggest that God inflicts retributive punishment. This leads us directly to the doctrine about indulgences, which since the activities of Tetzel were the occasion for Luther's protest against the shrunken god of popular Catholicism, has loomed large on the Roman Catholic charge sheet.

An indulgence ought only to be the application of the

truth that since we are all members of the Mystical Body of Christ, our prayer, which is Christ's prayer, our holiness, which is Christ's holiness, can assist—in some way beyond rational analysis—those who are suffering because they are not yet ready to share God's life. Beyond rational analysis. As soon as this idea is worked out in any detail what once appeared to be sound becomes doubtful; as soon as rules are drawn up for its practical application what once seemed sane becomes ridiculous. Shorn of extravagances, Catholics are taught that after God has forgiven the guilt of a sin, the temporal punishment (punishment which, unlike that endured in hell, will have an end) due to that sin is not invariably expiated in full either by the 'penance' the priest gives in Confession or good works and mortifications. Fortunately 'a potent remedy for or solvent of the punishment due to sin' is granted by ecclesiastical authority from the treasury of the accumulated merits of the saints entrusted to the Church for her disposal. These remittances or indulgences apply to the living and the dead; to the dead because they are offered to God in the hope that he will apply them to suffering souls; to the living that they may be absolved from punishment. These remittances may be partial or plenary, personal, real, or local.

With one exception, the Crusade Indulgence which can be bought in Spain for a small sum (together with a dispensation to eat meat on Friday), indulgences can no longer be paid for in money. But it was ungrateful of the Elector of Saxony of all people to support Luther. For in his castle he had relics the veneration of which earned 'the remission of 127,799 years, without reckoning quarantines.' To this day Catholics are told that such and such a prayer, the recitation of the rosary (provided the beads are held in the hand), the wearing of medals, visits to certain shrines, churches or cemeteries and many other pious actions will earn them, under certain conditions too complicated to be verified, the remission of a particular number of years, weeks, or days. To explain that these approximate to mediaeval penances is to miss the point. What was, in essentials, a profound insight has been degraded into superstitious practice by latin legalism and the Roman tendency to build a huge structure on inadequate foundations.

So it is that the Catechism can mention the advantages accruing to those who wear the Brown Scapular of Our Lady of Mount Carmel which was revealed to her by St. Simon Stock (at Cambridge). This is a reference to the famous 'Sabbatine Privilege', indulgences which depend on this apparition, now known to be an invention, but confirmed by several popes right up to Pius XI. 'The Scapular of Our Lady of Mount Carmel', writes Fr. H. Davis in his text-book on Moral and Pastoral Theology, 1938, 'carries many great indulgences. It is piously believed that this scapular will save from hell those who wear it till death, and will deliver them from purgatory at least on the Saturday after death.' Of the hair-splittings, qualifications, evasions, and bizarre conjectures which the doctrine of indulgences has given rise to, we will say nothing further save that they are no more relevant to religion than is a recipe compounded of herbs and crushed snails to the cure of tuberculosis.

'Unless a man is born of water and the Holy Ghost he cannot enter the kingdom of heaven.' No one now takes these words of Christ literally. It would be fair to say, however, that whatever its residual beliefs and credal statements, in practice the Roman Church is the only considerable communion left in the west to go on teaching that unbaptized babies and young children are so possessed by the devil that they are incapable of the Beatific Vision. Just as, to be effective, reformers must wear blinkers, so the infancy of any movement of thought obtains part of its drive from an intolerance and exclusiveness its later self regards as fanatical. There is no sign of any ecumenical spirit in the Acts and the Epistles; if there had been it is doubtful if the young church would have made much progress. But time slowly achieves what Carlyle called the 'exodus from Houndsditch', that is, the escape from antiquated forms of thought. Grudgingly and through clenched teeth Rome had to concede that actual membership of the visible church was not necessary for salvation; she had to develop a theory of baptism of desire;[1] she is now trying to extricate herself from an entirely orthodox doctrine which, since the term baby includes foetuses and those which die before full term (not to speak of all other unbaptized persons dying before the age of reason), deprives the vast majority of the human race from seeing God for all eternity. This superstition is hardly mitigated by the invention of limbo.

The decree of the Council of Florence which stated, 'the souls of those who depart this life in actual mortal sin, or original sin alone, go down to hell, but the penalty to which they will be subjected will be very different indeed', however humanely intended, perpetuates the superstition that God punishes retributively, that there is a distinction between the loss of the Beatific Vision and the actual pains he, in his justice, inflicts on sinners. Rome is here contradicting the deepest of her spiritual convictions. She knows well that it is impossible for human beings to be happy if they are to be prevented from enjoying the very end for which they have been created. But her theologians, unlike Protestants, are

---

[1] This was not originally developed with any regard to the salvation of non-Christians but only to meet the case of catechumens dying before baptism, therefore, of course, explicitly desiring it.

free only to arrive at such conclusions as are, superficially at any rate, consistent with orthodoxy. So, while anxious priests are considering the matter and flustered pastors are wondering how to explain to their flock that what they have been told before to be the revealed word of God has turned out to be an exploded idea about him, the old machinery grinds on.

It would be idle to pretend that the ordinary Catholic gives a moment's thought to the souls of Neanderthal infants playing with bones in the dimness of some semi-celestial cave, but they are terrified of condemning their own children to limbo, and of themselves being separated from them for ever. So priests successfully hustle babies to the font, they baptize embryos, foetuses, and still-born infants, cause enormous and superstitious distress to parents by refusing Christian burial to those who have escaped their attentions, and flip over theological manuals to find out if, in cases of malpresentation, baptism on the leg is sufficient to ensure eternal life.

This last superstition, that a sacrament is not valid unless certain approved words and gestures are exactly repeated, is not peculiar to baptism. It is shared by all ceremonial religions whether Christian or not and is therefore part of a much larger context.

'Magic wants to get,' Evelyn Underhill wrote, 'mysticism wants to give—immortal and antagonistic attitudes which turn up under one disguise or another in every age of thought.' In theory this distinction is clear, in practice it is blurred. Religion so often lies uneasily between the two extremes, tossing in its unquiet search from side to side—at times to use God, then to love him, at times to get, at others to give.

Savages perform ritual dances to end a drought. Nuns carry a statue of Our Lady into the garden to ward off the rain which threatens to ruin the school bazaar.

Here the formula is different, the aim identical. Religion is being used in an attempt to control an insufficiently understood environment.[1] This is not to say that extravagances of popular piety may not be the expression of genuine faith and love, or that the magical apparatus which sometimes surrounds a sacrament and serves by sensible means to bring closer supra-sensible reality prevents that sacrament from being an instrument of grace.

Those Christians who smile at ceremonial and dismiss as mere superstition the notion that a sacrament can ever be an efficacious means of intensifying God's life in the soul are guilty of a superficial and bogus intellectualism. They fail to see that everything that is most real to them is expressed through externals, some of them as ceremonial, and as foolish to the outsider as those at which they scoff; they are blind to the value of symbolic ritual actions, repetitions, in opening up the human mind to those truths which lie beyond the petty and destructive analysis of the discursive reason; while if they go so far as to deny that holiness can be expressed through matter they are forgetting that the Word became Flesh.

However, when all this has been said, it must be admitted that Rome, in her general teaching and practice, has often so degraded the sacraments that for a large number of Catholics they are regarded as something in the nature of spells. This is not only because, up to now, they have been conducted in a language which is gibberish to most of the participants, but because, in a misdirected effort to secure certainty of function, far too much emphasis has been laid on correct performance and far too little on the response of the recipient which

[1] A nineteenth century Dominican breviary contains an elaborate service to exorcise the demons who produce a storm and compel them to remove the storm clouds to barren and wild places where tempest and deluge of rain can do no harm.

—except in the case of baptism where this response is given not personally but by the faith of the whole Church —alone makes a sacrament fruitful.

The sacraments have no legitimate existence at all unless they act as instruments to increase and intensify the life of God in the soul. But, whatever the distinctions of the more accurate theologians, the delicate minuet played by the separation, the manoeuvering, the bringing together of *opus operatum* and *opus operantis*, the average Roman Catholic is conditioned to think of God's grace as channelled through pipes. They alone are on the mains. Experience forces them to perceive that others have private systems, but since these were not included in the original plan of the architect and were connected in spite of the warnings of the local council, they are uncertain, dangerous, and likely to be polluted. Of these Roman Catholic pipes seven were instituted by Christ and are fool-proof provided certain words or gestures are carried out, not necessarily either with reverence or intelligibility but correctly, that is, in accordance with the book of words.

What injects superstition into Roman sacramental practice is not the ceremonies surrounding the sacrament, repeated gestures, incantations, lights, exorcisms which inhabit the dim border country between mystery and magic. On the contrary, these things are one aspect of the richness of her tradition, the universality of her appeal, and although they are under attack from the neopuritans from within the Church herself, constitute an integral part of the whole of her ritual worship including the central act of the Mass. The superstition is that of *threskeia*—an obsession with a technical, mechanical validity which leads the Church to ask and to answer entirely wrong questions, and show by the very fact that they are considered seriously at all that she still has at least half a leg in Houndsditch, and that with part of her mind she is continuing the futile attempt to capture, monopolize, and manipulate God's grace.

Priests learn that baptism is invalid if administered with unmelted snow or hail, with oil, saliva, wine, tears, milk, sweat, beer or soup. They read that if there is a thick coating of lipstick there would be grave danger that the anointing of the mouth would not be complete and in that event the validity of the sacrament of Extreme Unction would be rendered doubtful. The mere fact of Catholic baptism, even if it is not known and whatever the intention of the parties, makes the sacrament of matrimony performed outside the Church invalid. The consecration at Mass takes no effect unless meticulous regulations about the kind of wine used are observed. Water mixed with the wine would probably not be changed at the consecration if it were poured in after the beginning and before the completion of the form of words; these words would be ineffective if the verb were omitted or the pronoun altered. Here is world of the wizard. Fortunately this superstitious the answer to the vexed question of what is valid and what is licit is dissolving before the practical difficulty which faces Roman Catholics when they come to consider the Protestant Eucharist. No one can think that the Elizabethan bishops intended to ordain sacrificing priests. Leo XIII therefore, in a decision which, to quote his own words, is 'perpetually fixed, ratified and irrevocable' declared Anglican orders to be null and void. Life contradicts that kind of logic. Romans who now recognize that Protestants possess a very real sacramental life are hard put to account for this convincingly within the terms of that part of their theology still stranded in Houndsditch, the *reductio ad absurdum* of which has been reached by the suggestion that in the shared churches of the future double tabernacles should be constructed with the Anglican host reserved on one side, the Roman Catholic on the other.

Much water has flowed under Lambeth Bridge since Sydney Smith could casually refer to the 'nonsense of the real presence' without fear of contradiction. Augustine remarks on the human weakness of 'trying to utter in speech to the sense of man what is grasped in the secret places of the mind'. A truth almost impossible to put into words without falling off the knife-edge which separates materialistic understanding on the one hand from explanations which would rid it of much of its content on the other, means that most people will lose their balance. On each side of any dispute what is being defended may be only half understood and that half crudely expressed and unintelligently expounded. In the bitterness and heat of the reforming day the attacks on the traditional doctrine of the Eucharist became just as coarse and superficial as were the assertions of its defenders, with the result that both were left in possession of a field not strictly theirs. But heretical tradesmen no longer say that spiders and toads are superior to the consecrated host, nor do church thieves boast like a Lollard of eating nine gods for their supper. In actual fact the difference between Roman Catholics and all but an extreme wing of their fellow Christians in this matter is one of terminology, emphasis, and above all, habits of devotion. Catholics have an unbroken tradition that Christ is really present in the Sacrament, the very vitality of which conviction is paid for in the crudities of popular piety which may degenerate into superstition among simple people. Palermo is not Potters Bar.

An uneducated clergy means an uneducated laity. It is a fault of mistaken religious teaching which produced a popular modern vision of an angel holding the chalice with a host on it dripping blood into the cup. This is an unfortunate extension into our own time bad mediaeval theology, against the materialism of of which the reformers so rightly protested. It is to be regretted that although instructed Roman Catholics would not go so far as to think they 'could see God made and eaten all day long' many are still taught to think and speak as if this mystery were intended to express not the sacramental presence of the risen Christ, but a miraculous priestly re-creation of his now non-existent earthly body. Further, it cannot be denied that despite Aquinas' warning that Christ is in the Sacrament '*non tamquam in loco sed tamquam in sacramento*' many Catholics, encouraged by faulty education, poor quality sermons, and devotional manuals, do tend to think of Christ himself being confined to the tabernacle, as being 'carried' by the priest, and actually moving in procession. But in a mystery so hard to conceptualize these things are venial. Even the sometimes sentimental religiosity of separate tabernacle devotions emphasize the truth of Christ's continued sacramental presence and make Roman Catholic churches living places of prayer not only on Sunday but every day of the week. This is in contrast to so many Protestant churches whose clergy and people have allowed these 'helps to heaven' to be obliterated from their religious lives with the result that, as a Presbyterian has himself pointed out, their churches often have an air of desolation and gloom artificially created by Catholics only on Good Friday.

Chesterton referred somewhere to 'the strongest and unmistakable mark of madness, the combination between a logical completeness and a spiritual contradiction.' Far graver than any abuse which may result from a too materialistic theology of the Eucharist is the typical Roman habit of surrounding the mystery with rules, regulations, and superstitious taboos. Women, worthy to receive it on their tongue, may not touch the chalice or host with their fingers; if a host accidentally falls on the hand the hand must be washed; if a host falls on the ground the spot must be cleansed with a moistened purificator; should consecrated wine be spilt the rubric bids the priest to lick it up with his tongue, or if this is too difficult the place must be scraped and the scrapings burnt; while if any fall on altar cloth or vestment, triple ablutions are prescribed to be performed over a chalice. This worm's eye view of the mystery of faith, utterly at variance with the spiritual depth of so much of the Church's teaching on the subject, is paralleled by the superstitious minutiae of the regulations which govern the Eucharist fast.

Because food or drink is defined as something taken exteriorly, it is not a violation of the fast to swallow blood from the gums or teeth, but it is a violation to swallow blood flowing from a cut on the lips or a finger; biting of nails does not effect the fast but biting off and swallowing of finger skin might do so, if the particles were more than the smallest and not mixed with saliva; within the prescribed time the eating of straw or green branches is forbidden, but it is permitted to enjoy human hair, dry wood, paper, and fruit stones provided they are cleansed of all pulp and deprived of the kernel. It is hard to believe that a religion whose priests approve, print, and propagate such superstitious rubbish can possibly be the same as that which has by its practice and teaching brought the transcendent God closer to the hearts and minds of millions.

The Test Act of 1678 declared that 'invocation of the Virgin Mary or any other saint, and the sacrifice of the Mass as they are now used in the Church of Rome, are superstitious and idolatrous.' Since on quite other grounds we have released Cranmer, Latimer, and Ridley from that unpleasant place once so confidently assigned to them, it is our turn to give approbation to their painful exercise of erroneous conscience and enjoy the echo of that laughter which must be reverberating about the courts of heaven as these three look down on the efforts of modern Roman Catholics to re-present and reform the Mass. What with the turnings round and moving about of altars, zealous references to vulgar tongues, Holy Tables, the Lord's Supper, Common Meals and Services of Commemoration, these Protestant martyrs must be wondering if the halcyon days of Edward VI have not returned. It is self-evident then that many Roman Catholics themselves feel there is need for some radical change of emphasis in the Mass, but even as it now stands—and it will soon be changed— it contains no hint of superstition or idolatry. The same cannot be said of the cult of the Blessed Virgin and the saints, although this, in its turn, has been misunderstood frequently by those who do not share it, and mis-stated by those who do.

The Communion of Saints is only another way of expressing that solidarity of the human race to which we have already referred. That is, provided their wills are turned in love to a God whom they may not even recognize, all human beings whether alive or dead are united in his life. That the Church first restricted this life to her own members, then to other Christians, and now does not know quite what to think, illustrates the slow emergence of any religion from its infant egoism. This solidarity can be expressed by sharing the sufferings of others, by praying for them, by praying to them. Not I live, but Christ lives in me. Since God's life in humanity is himself incarnate, there is no question of the saints 'coming between us and him', of praying to the saints

33

instead of 'going directly to God'. Our prayer, the
saints' prayer, Christ's prayer, are one and the same.
If a Catholic addresses his prayer to a saint it is only a
different way of approaching God, not a halting place
on the road to him. The objection that it is superstitious
and degrading to suggest that human beings can mediate
between us and God surely shows a defective understanding of the Incarnation.

The Church preaches to Greek and barbarian,
learned and simple. One day, if the world survives, a
certain mediocre standard of education will be universal.
The difficulty at the moment is that there are particular
areas, for example in the industrialized west, where the
majority of people have reached this standard, but there
are other, larger, areas where the mass of the people are
barbarians. In the past, faced with almost universal
barbarism, the Church of Rome had to adapt her teaching to the understanding of her hearers, with the result
that many silk purses were turned into sow's ears.
This happened with the cult of the saints, so that even
educated Catholics are caught up in attitudes of mind
and thought processes which now only belong to
Mediterranean peasants and Mexican peons. That is to
say they sometimes speak of the saints in the manner of
field labourers since the world began, making them
tutelary spirits of themselves capable of curing tooth-
ache, finding lost property, or ensuring safe childbirth.
This leads to many semi-superstitious tricks of devotion,
the pinning on of medals and scapulars as a protection
against harm, bargaining with the saints, and, as of old
an image of Isis paid a ceremonial visit to Syria, carrying
statues of saints from place to another. In this manner
the Madonna of Fatima was recently transported by
air to Frankfurt to enjoy a six-week tour of the archdio-
cese of Cologne.

These things, however, though they are silly, and bring the whole idea of devotion to the saints into disrepute, are superficial abuses. When people pray to the saints they pray to God incarnate in his creatures. If popular practice sometimes suggests that the saints can help, so to speak, independently of God, this is to be deplored. Nevertheless, the mere fact of such prayer, however imperfectly understood, protects the profound truth that God has deified humanity in identifying it with himself. Moreover, devotion to the saints expressed by feast-days, pictures, and statues is a genuine means of presenting spiritual reality in a manner more readily grasped; of forming a bridge between one kind of experience and another, and, by animating heroic love, assisting people to live more unselfish lives themselves. Blanket condemnations of other people's habits of devotion are not only arrogant but unwise. One would not suppose the religious atmosphere at *Les Buissonnets* to be exactly invigorating yet it produced St Thérèse and certainly other very holy people. The weakness of reforming movements is that they make the best the enemy of the good. A completely pure religion for the few would be no religion for the many. The Protestants' comparative neglect of the world of sense in their worship has impoverished and devitalized it. They have been too often 'guiltily and meanly dead' to the way human beings may be reached through the eyes as well as through the intellect; imagined sermons have a greater spiritual value then concrete imagery.

When all is said and done a great deal of complaint about Roman Catholic devotion to the saints is more of an historical grudge than a real objection. The fact that a single child can die in pain is far more of a scandal of the faith of a Christian than any of the irregularities which have been mentioned. The God of Abraham did not save his people at Belsen, and for the victims of the allies at Dresden Christ and his saints slept. A generation which is bitterly and acutely conscious of the sufferings of good, innocent, and praying people, is no longer concerned about the purest form of petitionary prayer but with the value of that kind of prayer at all. This question, involving as it does the nature of evil, faces all Christians, in fact all human beings who believe in a God of love. It can be answered neither by pious platitudes nor angry rejection, but perhaps best by those who have never asked it, whose faith transcends the superficially irreconcilable because it is rooted in those depths of the spirit where lives God himself.

Responsible Roman Catholics today are well aware of the dangers and decadence of some of the devotional language used about Our Lady. While there is no need to defend the positive side of a cult which has done so much to illuminate God's self-disclosure to man, its exaggerations have tended to obscure the very truth which alone gave it meaning. The lop-sidedness of popular Catholicism in this respect is superstitious because in practice it makes a creature play a bigger part in the thought and worship of an individual than God himself who recedes, a shadowy remote figure, into the background. That this figure is terrible as well as remote, so that blasphemy is added to superstition, is due to the quirk of an entirely false development by means of which a distinction came to be made between the mercy of Our Lady (or the other saints) and the justice of God. This mistake which all Christians sometimes have made when describing the relationship of Christ to the Father,[1] implies that Our Lady or the saints are somehow softer hearted, that is,

[1] It was this kind of thinking which gave Matthew Arnold an opportunity in *Literature and Dogma* to make some of his most effective jibes.

36

more full of love, than God himself. The Blessed Virgin can get round her Son, a saint particularly close to God can drop a soothing word in his dreadful and terrible ear. St Bernard could say, 'let him who fears the Son take refuge in Mary', and it is extremely unfortunate that these totally unworthy notions are given wide currency in modern times by the popularization of certain kinds of apparitions. Whereas other people in the world besides Roman Catholics have visions, the Catholic Church is the only large group which makes systematic use of them for dogmatic and devotional purposes.

Although no Christian can logically say that God has never revealed himself through abnormal psychic phenomena, innumerable theological and psychological problems arise when their nature is considered. These notorious difficulties cannot be discussed in themselves but, it must be admitted, the charge that Roman Catholic authorities have glossed them over has some justification.

When the Catholic Church is good she is very very good; when she is bad she is horrid. Perhaps nowhere are the two sides of Roman Catholicism (felt so sharply by Newman on his first visit to Italy) shown more clearly than in the unequal spiritual value of the visions her members have experienced and in her attitude towards these experiences. The classic mystics whose perceptions of God are the very life-blood of Christianity frequently experienced abnormal visual or auditory phenomena. Yet they are the people who warn us most severely against attaching importance of any kind to visions. 'Though they may happen to the bodily senses in the way of God,' writes St John of the Cross, 'we must never delight in them nor encourage them; yea, rather we must fly from them without seeking to know whether their origin be good or evil. For inasmuch as they are

37

exterior or physical, the less the likelihood of their being from God.' This is the one voice of Rome, the voice which is sanely conscious that although visions may indeed be a way in which God enlightens a human mind, they are at best an imperfect and untrustworthy method of apprehending him. When this voice is uttered Catholics are taught that, while they may not deny the possibility of such occurrences, no one is bound, *de fide*, to believe in the Divine origin of any particular vision, nor—commendable caution when we remember that St Catherine of Siena thought that the Blessed Virgin revealed that she was not conceived immaculate—does she 'guarantee' the content of any special revelation whatsoever.

The other voice is the voice of the salesman, the pedlar of package-piety, of religious ready-mix. It implies that as long as a sufficient number of fairly respectable people believe in a supposed revelation it is temerarious, impious, and distinctly un-Catholic to doubt its truth. This voice encourages the faithful to seek for signs and wonders, to admire the miraculous element in the lives of the saints, to thirst for visions, and what is worse, to believe that these manifestations are in themselves objective, and not symbolic of transcendent reality. This leads people into materialistic piety of the grossest kind. They are encouraged to think that St Anthony actually held the child Jesus in his arms, that a holy nun really played ball with him in the choir, that devils appear in the form of dogs, and archangels shake their golden curls. When this kind of literalism is applied to auditory phenomena it can lead to superstition and blasphemy.

Whatever the real nature of the experiences of the children at Fatima in 1917 (and it would seem that these contain nothing that is not traceable to their—woefully inadequate—religious training), the appearances there of Our Lady, St Joseph, and the Child Jesus are renowned the world over. Solar miracles have been reported, a huge basilica built, thousands of pilgrims visit the spot every year, and Pope Pius XII himself was favoured with similar visions in the very gardens of the Vatican. Since the subjects' original statement has 'for prudential reasons' never been made public, and Roman Catholic scholars admit that a great deal in the devotional literature dealing with the matter has been suppressed, altered, and generally touched up, any comment on the dogmatic content of these visions must be provisional. But one can say it is a pity they were not treated with more reserve, and a disaster if a single soul has been led to think that God in any way resembles the dreadful and cruel being suggested by the words of the apparition.

The visions of the children at Fatima and the mystical experiences of St Margaret Mary Alacoque are entirely different. For St Margaret Mary's vision of the Sacred Heart, despite the language in which it is clothed and the pathological disorders of the subject, are symbolic of a profound truth—the infinite love of God shown in the humanity of Christ. But they have one thing in common. By allowing both visions to be understood in a materialistic way Rome has encouraged the taking out of fire insurance policies on a large scale. At Fatima Our Lady blackmails people into making the devotion of the First Saturdays, that is by going through certain hoops they will obtain assistance at the hour of death, 'such as is necessary for eternal bliss'. The Christ of St Margaret Mary's vision urges Catholics to believe that all who take communion on the first Friday of any consecutive month (if one is omitted, the course must start again) will not only receive the Last Sacraments before their death but their eternal salvation will be absolutely secured.

Yet it must be noted that the very people who believe

and try to convince others that the words of certain apparitions are literally dictated by Christ, themselves exhibit an odd lack of confidence in his word. The Sacred Heart nun, Josefa Menendez, experienced lengthy revelations which have been widely publicized. 'Josefa,' we are told, 'writes down His words exactly as they come from the Divine mouth.' But Karl Rahner, S.J., points out that the German edition of these revelations took care to omit both the information that the robe Christ's mother made for him as a child miraculously grew with him, and the directive to Josefa to hate her criminal and accursed flesh. Perhaps the editors were nervous lest God's words should spoil their chances of obtaining an *imprimatur*.

Surely all revelation of a transcendent God must, without exception, in the nature of the case, be filtered through the human intellect and human understanding, coloured by the imagination of the recipient, and distorted by language not fitted to express it. A creative artist communicates his perceptions of truth and beauty through physical media, but these are only symbolic of that interior grasp of reality which exists in his mind, and inevitably fall far short of it. It is the same with those people who undoubtedly experience God through abnormal psychic activity, and as according to his capacity and mood the artist's work is closer or further from reality, so is the visionary's perception of Supreme Being. If, instead of making use of these experiences in the manner of a circus promoter, conjurer, or quack, the Church would be true to her better voice and insist that they are but an oblique and frequently unreliable method of apprehending God, so much of what is of abiding spiritual value would cease to be dismissed as absurd. Nor would Catholics lay themselves open to well-founded charges of superstition and credulity.

If contradictory apprehensions of the nature of God may exist in the same person (as they exist in the same religious tradition) and such a man shows all the signs of holiness, how much more may holiness exist with the far less radical error of credulity. Education is a slow process; in certain societies credulity may be a necessary accompaniment of faith. As long as the barbarians continue to outnumber the Greeks, the simple the learned, in practice the worship of God is bound to be a compromise. No country develops at the same rate. In some parts of the world religious theory may be well in advance of the religious practice of the majority. In others the practice—or what the majority really think—may be in advance of traditional theory. At this point the sin of making a virtue of credulity is mortal.

To an extent which would have horrified the little group gathered round Johnson at Oxford, Christianity as they understood it has ceased to be an intellectually credible explanation of the world. Today all reflecting Christians know they are fighting with their backs to the wall. Yet a great many ecclesiastical authorities seem unaware of this, or are under the singular impression that because once a handful of geese saved the Capitol it is their duty to imitate those obliging birds. The Catholic equivalent of 'not before the servants' is to mutter about the simple faith of pious washerwomen. If the clergy in the more developed countries did their own laundry they would know that washerwomen, pious or otherwise, no longer exist. Father Philip Hughes was more realistic. Writing a quarter of a century age, he complained of those who, while offering a young mind knowledge in secular subjects commensurate with his maturity, would leave him in the matter of revealed truths with the intellectual formation of a boy. Catholics in school and parish are encouraged to believe not only facts which most certainly have not been revealed, but many which are clean contrary to what their secular knowledge tells them to be true.

This deliberate fostering of credulity takes many forms and is to be found in the highest places. The Fathers of the Vatican Council, to the scandal surely of the non-Catholic observers, are to be invited to venerate a head of St Andrew for whose authenticity there is not a tittle of evidence. In a public ceremony an English bishop can receive an old bit of cloth to be honoured as a fragment of Our Lady's veil. Nuns who intelligently and devotedly coach their brighter pupils in the hope that they will carry the lamp of Catholic truth into the university suggest that the picture before which they pray for success is a copy of one painted by angels. Students who in their secular work are debating the existence of *homo habilis* are informed in their religious textbook that Adam and Eve were 'very splendid people' with beautiful and healthy bodies preserved from all forms of illness. They are told that from the time of the Apostles Christians have believed in the bodily assumption of the Blessed Virgin, and that her Immaculate Conception has always been the general belief of the Church confirmed by apparitions of Our Lady herself. Their Catechism is a mixture of bronze-age theology and biblical fundamentalism[1] seasoned by some pious falsehoods. Catholic Truth Society pamphlets, which the hierarchy exhort the laity to read in order to become theologically literate, include some of the highest standard, but too many are of doubtful value, while others repeat discredited fables in edition after edition. It is a pity that a better example is not given from above,

[1] Such as that the return of Elias and Enoch will prelude the end of the world, and that the Last Judgement will be held in the valley of Josaphat.

that exploded legends still remain in the breviary, that Leo XIII in a papal bull could go so far as to recount the whole story of the discovery of the supposed body of St James the Great at Compostela and to affirm as authentic the Apostles's remains. We must be sorry that a Church which has so valiantly maintained that religious truth is not just the guess of a worm in the dust should so persistently throw dust in people's eyes.

Whether out of stupidity or consciousness of shared guilt the opponents of Rome sometimes attack her at her strongest point and are blind to those places where she is most vulnerable. The accusation that her members worship images is foolish, and Protestant touchiness on this point is a fad, the mere nursing of a preparatory school grievance. But there is a sense in which it is fair to say that Roman Catholics worship idols, and the very idols which their true selves repudiate.

The Marxist looks forward to the withering away of the state, the Catholic to the withering away of the Church when the kingdom of God is fully revealed. Yet, in the manner of her arch-enemy, Rome has exalted an organization which exists solely to bring men to God through prayer into a sinless abstraction, an idol which protects itself by means of repressive machinery and is as neurotically sensitive to criticism as if it were some mushroom sect and not the Church which Macaulay admitted to be great and respected before the Saxon set foot in Britain and the Frank had passed the Rhine. Such exercise of authority as is necessary for the protection of truth and the securing of decent order is too often employed to preserve an untarnished official image, while in the legitimate religious sphere, although the rights of conscience have been affirmed, its exercise has been stifled and the dissonant voice silenced by means of excommunications, sanctions, secret delations, clerical oaths, and circulated lists of suspect persons. St Ignatius remarked[1] that if the Church told him what seemed purely white was black he would pronounce it black. Fortunately this language—reminiscent of a totalitarian People's Court—is slowly going out of fashion, although many Catholics are still so accustomed to unthinking obedience that they are often incapable of judging a course of action on its own merits. They have been conditioned to hold a sacerdotal caste in such respect that they frequently deserve the charge of being so superstitiously priest-ridden that they will believe anything as long as it comes from the mouth of pope, bishop, or clerk.

Ever since the Church came under the protection of the State almost all religious authorities—save where their own interests were concerned—have supported Caesar in any war he may have chosen to wage. They have encouraged their flock not only to burn incense before the idol of national sovereignty but to offer themselves as living sacrifices in its defence. This policy reached its logical climax in the appalling record of the German bishops during the last war. Without minimizing the real difficulties of the situation, it should be remarked that it is still continued by those Roman Catholics in authority the world over who, while preaching the Christian life, do not dare to suggest to those under their charge that it might be wrong to massacre their fellow human beings on a colossal scale.

In the same sense that the Jews made gods of their bellies by inventing an elaborate food code, so Roman theologians have made gods of the human reproductive organs. This well known obsession would be tedious to discuss. But it can be put into perspective by pointing out that if contraceptives had been dropped over Japan

[1] *Exercises. Rules for thinking with the Church.*

instead of bombs which merely killed, maimed, and shrivelled up thousands alive, there would have been a squeal of outraged protest from the Vatican to the remotest Mass centre in Alaska.

All these idols, however, are being gradually discredited by the spirit now renewing the face of the Church. Roman Catholics must have faith that the next generation will feel the need only of explaining what they no longer wish to defend.

Within such a short space it has not been possible to do more than to pull out one or two discoloured threads from a tangled and ageless skein. Rome should not be outlawed because she continues to sanction superstitions once part of the belief of every Christian, nor should she be sneered at because she tolerates credulity where it is a necessary accompaniment of any faith at all. But if in its place the peasant's god is harmless, the shrunken god of Houndsditch, the god of the rubric, the canon lawyer, and the curial official is always and everywhere deadly. If credulity must sometimes be ignored, credulity deliberately cultivated for the sake of prestige or edificacation is indefensible. These last are the root of the evil, the source of serious scandal, the reason why people who would be Papists if they could so often find themselves unable to join the Church. But it is by no means the whole story.

Queen Elizabeth I 'dispersed the buyers and sellers of Popish trash, the stumbling-stones of superstition, the monuments of idolatry and vanity.' Yet she was willing and eager to consult the astrologer Dr Dee about a wax image of her royal person found most alarmingly with pins stuck in it near Lincoln's Inn Fields. Because man does not know the laws which govern his life he invents them; because he is conscious of the inadequacy of his inventions he distrusts them, turning in trapped awareness from one hypothesis to another. Since human weakness and ignorance placed God where he does not belong, imprisoned him within a system of thought exploded by scientific knowledge, man turned to worship those who destroyed this ancient image, to find not only that science cannot protect him because it does not pretend to know the nature of matter or the limits of the possible, but that its terms of reference simply do not include those things most vital for the human spirit. Foiled on one side he will return to Dr Dee or pay large sums for a piece of magic bark;[1] foiled on the other his aspirations will curdle into a sour humanism. And this is the heart of the matter.

The stupidities, the absurdities of the Roman Catholic Church are there for all to see, Aunt Sallies which any half-educated lout may shatter with a twist of his animal arm. But the lout does not know that he has been deluded into believing something far more deeply absurd, false, and silly than any broken image which lies grinning on the ground. He has been guilty of that superstition which the Greeks recognized, a too great unbelief, a negative credulity just as gross and far more damaging than its counterpart. He has been seduced by his environment into thinking that the only things which can be true are those which are capable of empirical proof, persuaded that nothing lies beyond the range of rational demonstration. So he denies to religion what he unconsciously affirms every day of his life when he loves another human being or admires the flowers in his garden.

To any one who may have taken offence at some of the remarks contained in this essay a final reflexion may

[1] A man has made as much as a thousand pounds a week from the sale of pieces of bark from a lucky cork oak. See interview in *News of the World*, May 31st, 1964.

serve as an explanation and apology. 'It is', wrote St
Paul, 'by making the truth publicly known that we
recommend ourselves to the honest judgement of mankind.' This is the task of the writer on Catholic theology
or history, to discharge which faithfully he should
surely combine the attitudes both of Voltaire, and St
John of the Cross. Of Voltaire to dissolve with the acids
of ridicule and sarcasm the all too human aspects of
belief and practice which a human religion must inevitably assume but which must be scoured away when a
changed intellectual climate has rendered them incredible; of St John, to keep his intellect attentive to the
underlying truths of the spirit, eternal and immutable
because they issue from the depths of God and speak to us
of Himself.

The Worldly Church

Political Bias, Autocracy and Legalism

JOHN M. TODD

THERE is a danger of arguing these objections purely on a plane of high theory. Often enough an 'objection' as held by a particular person is closely tied in either with quite concrete experiences, or at least with a picture of people or occasions or things which typify it. Probably the leaders of the Conservative party and the Labour party respectively become such images of much that members of the opposite party specially dislike. Religious beliefs often run stronger than political convictions; the 'wrong' religion is then thought of as identical with some picture in the mind, which takes on a specially undesirable or evil character in the objector's mind. There is a risk, in adverting to such symbols, of distorting the real objection, the thought which lies at the heart of the horror. But our task here is first of all to state an objection as it is in an objector's mind. The typical symbol of this 'worldly' church needs to be put before our eyes. Here it is then.

The cardinals, the bishops, the monsignori, dressed in their varieties of red, scarlet and glorious magenta (the ancient Roman *purpureus*), the prelates, moving swiftly or slowly, austerely or humanly, strictly or kindly, in some social gathering: they are a striking cross-section of humanity with their very different origins and their very different expressions. But they have one indelible quality—'authority'. They are men to be respected. Some with vast power; some with little power. And back behind them, somewhere in the Vatican, is the Pope, immaculate, white—authority incarnate. In any such gathering dressed according to protocol, the prelates represent what many of the Fathers of the Second Vatican Council, in their effort to be rid of this fatal something, have called 'triumphalism'. What lies behind the image might be expressed thus: 'Christ has founded his Church with its centre in Rome, and it shall survive, in its glory, the instrument of the Holy Spirit, until the end of time'. This triumphal spirit has for many centuries activated more or less consciously the 'authoritative' attitude of Catholic prelates, the dressing up, the protocol, what for want of a better word we sometimes call the 'feudal' traditions in the Church. Seeking to exercise what they think of as the Church's rightful power, indeed the Church's duty to rule in Christ's name, over all things and all men, the Church's prelates have striven to see that the Church is always present 'in the world', on all suitable occasions, with a certain air of authority, sometimes restrained, sometimes strongly asserted, according to the tactical needs of the moment. And 'the Church' has always meant simply the cardinals, bishops and other prelates; the ordinary priest is present only as representing one of these; and the laity are not only not eligible as representatives, they have been, on the contrary, commonly thought of, in these perspectives, as a danger to 'the Church'. They are the 'world' in which the 'Church' has to be present, the 'State' which the 'Church' must influence. This then is the sense in which a picture of a gathering of prelates may be identified as the symbol of 'the worldly Church', to which objection is taken.

If this is a tradition which some prelates, perhaps many, perhaps very many, wish to dispense with, it is not one which they can easily doff. The majority of the laity still expect them to maintain it; the laity like to identify the 'dignity of the priesthood' with a special caste. It must demand a special effort, often enough, for a prelate to say 'No' to this old tradition, picturesque, popular, orderly (in appearance). It must be an effort to reject the excuses: 'Even if Christ never went about like this, all the same he meant his Church to and he would never have allowed his Church to build her great traditions if he did not approve'—and in such an idea lies the inadequate theology which is at the back of the trouble, but this theology is not our sphere in this chapter. It is clear that there is a strong movement to reject the old triumphal tradition. Many prelates are saying they wish not to rule in the old-fashioned sense but to serve, and they do conduct themselves both in public and private in a way which tallies with what they say. But the objection remains, for we are concerned with a tradition which is a thousand years old, and still very strong. Let us try to define it more precisely.

Should the Church, then, be 'other-wordly'? In a sense, yes. Christians are bound to the teachings of Jesus, and perhaps many other men of whatever conviction would agree with the ethical ideal which can be seen to be consonant with it: 'Seek first the Kingdom of God'.

But this is not an injunction to be 'other-worldly' in the sense in which it means leaving 'the world'. The objection with which I intend to deal is not the objection that Christianity is involved with everyday life, and that it should not be so involved; I am not dealing with the objection that Christianity ought to retreat from the world and does not do so. The call to perfection, to 'all goodness' (NEB), which is made in the Sermon on the Mount is a call to be good in a world not perfectly good. It is not a call to give up being a tax-gatherer (civil servant—in the employ of the foreign, pagan, occupying power) and shut oneself away and have nothing further to do with this difficult world and to think only of God. It is a call to be a good tax-gatherer (in conditions which many politicians and some Christian priests and ministers today would regard as virtually treasonable or sinful). It is a call which involves giving to Caesar what is Caesar's, and being willing to give him some of the coins he has made available. Christians can, and must, argue about the detail of this, in order to try to realize justice as perfectly as possible. What they cannot do is to say that Christ's words mean that the religious man must leave the world. They clearly cannot mean that. They must mean that Christians are bound to some social relationship with their fellows as a good thing. Christianity is a religion of charity, of love; its doctrine of the Holy Trinity is bound up with the belief that God the Son lived on earth as a man and that his spirit brings the life of God to all men in a great variety of ways within the normal run of everyday life.

The objection we are concerned with is that the Catholic Church, in accepting this involvement in the world, has institutionalized it. The gospel of truth and charity has, so the objection goes, been turned into a matter of rules and regulations. And in this guise it has.

it is said, deserved the terrible criticism which Jesus rained down on the Pharisees for their legalism. This legalistic and autocratic perversion is tied in with the political aspect, with the European tradition of 'Christian States'. In practice this European tradition has often meant that Christian authority, the authority of pope and bishops, has been used to support something which the State wished to enforce but which had little relevance to, and sometimes was definitely contradictory to, the Christian gospel. Or conversely the State was used to enforce the Church's own requirements, through undue influence and regardless of established political procedure, or simply to enforce standards which were no longer proper, either in a Christian or any other sense.

Of modern examples one thinks of those States where Catholicism is the State religion and Protestant worship has been forbidden or only barely tolerated. One thinks of the Italian legislation which has made any propaganda for birth regulation (by any method) illegal. Then there is conscientious objection; the States where Catholics have been in a majority are the last to recognize that conscientious objection is something other than treason. These are all modern examples. One hardly needs specific examples from earlier ages. The Papal State played a part in international politics like any other State. One result of this was that a whole region would sometimes be put under interdict and the sacraments withheld and Mass not allowed to be celebrated, on account of a quarrel between Rome and local political authority.

The objection we are dealing with tends to contrast the practice of the Catholic Church with the practice of the primitive Church in the first three centuries. The bad tradition is traced back to the time when Christianity became the official religion of the Roman Empire

53

following the conversion of Constantine. Whatever the exact truth about the first four centuries it is certain that as the Roman Empire was gradually circumscribed, attacked and occupied by the tribes, Christian bishops often took the lead in civil life, to try to preserve order, or to parley with the tribal leaders, and to work out a *modus vivendi*. And in Rome the Pope became at the same time the head of the State and the head of the Church.

From these historical facts grew up the twofold tradition of the political Church, to which objection is taken. Twofold because the Church was both involved with the State (and later the Universities) in maintaining a general *imperium*, or authority, and was also chronically at enmity with one particular State or another on various tactical matters, often far removed from specifically Christian considerations. There is a direct line of cause and effect from these facts to the present day States which are though of as embodying much of the substance of this objection, for instance Italy, Spain, and much of South America. These countries have, in the religious sphere, their good, charming and charitable aspects. The 'bad' side, which stems from the 'worldly' or 'political' tradition includes: their backwardness; the 'feudal' division between priests and people, the latter being those, as in the civil sphere, to whom things are done and administered; an unhistorical, static idea of the world simply as a sinful place where man is tested, and to the evils of which he must resign himself. No real effort then is made, at a political, economic and social level, to achieve justice for its own sake, or to provide the circumstances in which men may most happily fulfil themselves and practice charity. Indeed the argument tends to be turned the other way and it may be said that charity has the best opportunity to flourish in situations of disaster and injustice. And so the radical failure to attempt any improvement is justified. The result is a dead, almost a pre-Christian world, a world of fatalism and preternaturalism, a world where man's free choice is reduced to the barest minimum.

We have been describing the 'worldly' Church as part of a total social structure. What of the Church's own life? These worldly aspects were and are all of a piece with the Church's own internal life. It is part of the objection we are discussing that the Church has carried into every sphere of its own life this 'worldly', this 'feudal' way of dealing with every matter and with its own members. In a word the objection, as it relates to the Church's own internal life, is that Canon Law has been put in the place of the truth and charity of the gospel. In the place of morals and conscience stand rules and ecclesiastical authority. We are now at the heart, I think, of the objection. It is no myth thought up by the enemies of the Church. The facts are established and well known. They have been summarized by Père Congar, an eminent theologian, in their historical and doctrinal aspects. It will be in place to quote five paragraphs from his description of authority in the Church in the medieval period.[1]

'I believe however that the spirit of the time introduced something new . . . namely, a certain legalistic aspect.

'We see this legalism at work in the importance attached to the formal validity of authority, to its possession of a title in law. There is no insistence on the need of an actual intervention of God's grace, nor therefore on the need for man to pray for this

[1] *Problems of Authority* (London and Baltimore, 1962), edited by John M. Todd, pp. 139 *et seq.*

intervention and to prepare for it by bodily mortifica-
tion, by explicitly relating the exercise of authority to
sacred acts such as the celebration of the mysteries,
fasting, chastity, prayer, etc. In short, legalism is
characteristic of an ecclesiology unrelated to spiritual
anthropology, and for which the word *ecclesia* indicates
not so much the body of the faithful as the system, the
apparatus, the impersonal depositary of the system of
rights whose representatives are the clergy or, as it is
now called, the Hierarchy, and ultimately the Pope
and the Roman Curia.

'It is a fact that "Church" is sometimes understood
by the theorists of ecclesiastical power or papal
authority as indicating clerics, priests and the Pope.
This use of the word was completely unknown to the
Fathers and the liturgy. It is a fact that in a large
number of modern documents, the word 'Church'
indicates the priestly government or even quite
simply this government's Roman courts. It is distinct
from the faithful, from men in general and outside and
above them. Here is one example from hundreds which
could be given: "The Church is given the task of feed-
ing the flock of Jesus Christ".[1] But the Church is
herself this flock. This change of meaning is serious.
In the first place, it is out of keeping with scriptural,
patristic and liturgical usage. Further, it runs the
risk of separating the "Church" from the sphere in
which men are trained in the spiritual life. I would like
to point out in this respect a problem which, as far as
I know, has never been considered, namely the
application of the directives of the Gospel, not only
to individuals but to the Church as such. Is it the
individual alone who must be the servant and not the

[1] Mauro Capellari, in the opening address of his *Triomphe du
St-Siège et de l'Eglise* (trad. fr., t. 1, p. 18).

master, who must forgive offences, bless his enemies and not curse them? Have themes such as these any longer a place in an ecclesiology identified in practice with a treatise on public ecclesiastical law?

'Further, under these conditions, instead of being seen as a relationship of superior to subordinate *within* the vast system of mutual love and service between Christians who are Christians as a result of a grace for which each is accountable to all, does not authority run the risk of being posited *first and foremost* as *authority for its own sake,* and so of being looked upon in a purely juridical and socio-logical way, and not from a spiritual and Christian standpoint?

'It is obvious that Christians and men of God anxious to work for his Kingdom and devoid of all self-interest, have shaped their lives in accordance with this juridical concept. At a more prosaic level, this is true of conscientious churchmen. But it has favoured the growth of the idea of the priest as *governing* his parish, as exercising a *regimen,* as *regens.* It has favoured the growth of the idea of the bishop and the Pope as *judges,* of the Pope as a *Sovereign,* since he is the vicar of Christ, *Rex regum et Dominus dominantium.* It has favoured the growth of the idea of the Church as *Queen* of mankind, since she is the Bride of Christ who is the Ruler of the world. It cannot be denied that, from the eleventh century onwards, authority, and in particular the supreme authority of the Pope, borrowed many of the features of the vocabulary, insignia, ceremonial, style and ideology of the imper-ial court. These factors sometimes go back to pagan days and even, by way of the hellenistic monarchy of Alexander, to the Persian paganism of the fourth century B.C. Even the title of *Curia* assumed by the

papal administration was borrowed from the secular
vocabulary and, at the time, there were those who did
not fail to point this out.'

Does all this come to a special climax at some point of
practice? Is there some aspect which seems specially
scandalous to those who make objection? The most obvious point perhaps is the extent to which the Church
used imprisonment and torture on her own members in
matters of internal concern (the Spanish Carmelite
superiors had St John of the Cross in prison in the sixteenth century). In the same line is the capital punishment of heretics. The Church preferred not to be directly
responsible for death, but she judged a heretic and was a
party to that general *imperium* which then, through the
secular arm, committed the heretic to the flames. The
Church authorities, then, were quite happy to use
torture and violence short of death, and were prepared to
under-write the death penalty so long as someone else
put it into execution. Respect for the individual was not
really thought of by authority, by the great majority of
Catholic Christians, as a necessary corollary of the
gospel. The whole of the Church's life, in its majority
aspect, mirrors the description given by Père Congar.
It is hardly too much to speak of the ordinary members of
the Church, even including the parish priests, often
enough, as a proletariat; the liturgy which was the point
at which they all congregated together was a ritual of
which few of either priests or laity understood more than
a very small part of its Latin tongue, and whose sacramental and theological significance was hardly grasped
by most.

To all this objection it might be replied: 'You accuse
the Church of having an "unhistorical" idea of the
world. Your own objection is absurdly unhistorical in

the same sense. The facts you adduce are simple effects of known economic and political facts. There never was the slightest chance that anything but this development could have occurred following the break-up of the Roman Empire.' But this answer, though the economic and political factors need to be borne in mind, does not dispose of the objection, because it is precisely part of the Christian case that man can control his destiny on earth to some degree, that this world is not purely the result of material factors outside his control. On Christian grounds, then, Christian practice could indeed have been much better and much closer to that ideal which is to be found in the gospel. It need not and ought not to have become a mere matter of rules and regulations, a matter first and last of obedience.

Père Congar refers, in the final sentence of the piece we have quoted, to the Curia. And of course the Curia is the villain of the piece according to the case we are making. It is the Church's executive body, dealing at top level and from the centre, both with the Church's own affairs, and with its relations with all other human communities, including, and primarily, political communities; it has a 'Home Office' and a 'Foreign Office'. Obviously the existence of the Curia, or a similar body, was and is unavoidable. Individual bishops cannot control everything on a purely local basis. The Pope cannot by himself keep control of all matters, and must rely on someone to put his own decisions into effect. So the Church's civil service grew up, and within a short time it became a factor of great practical power. Its special character, however, emerged from the combination of this great day-to-day power with the conviction, based on the Church's theology, that God himself was likely to, or even certainly did, underwrite every decision and action of the Curia.

The members of the Curia then consider that they are administering the Church in God's name, and that they have the Holy Spirit to guide them. Their decisions became something which cannot be questioned, which must be right. Of course angry rulers or conscience-struck heretics did question them, but the absolute nature of the authority, and its assumption of quasi-divine or actually divine authenticity was what counted for the great majority of the Church's members. Once the assumption of this kind of authority had gone unchallenged it grew into a vast immobile complex of conventions, against which Luther first revolted successfully, but which then retrenched and became even more extreme. This power complex was often a very subtle combination of great practical ability and of personal courtesy, even charity. Within the power-complex the members of the Curia were able to go about their work with charm and unhurried graciousness, with the exercise often of a great deal of kindness. Commonly the members of the Curia might be said to be very intelligent, very 'reasonable' (within quite wide limits, and always willing to stretch a point, or two points; the velvet gloves are often many layers thick before the iron hand is reached), very quiet, very diplomatic. Kindness is perhaps the quality anyone might quite often experience. When one has absolute power, and when one believes that this power is really the final power in all human affairs, there is no doubt that a special ease can be achieved in one's relations with others. But a more or less unscrupulous harshness, even brutality, has often been experienced by those who do not yield.

Obviously in such a situation fearful corruption and abuse are possible. This is the case wherever men have power. *A fortiori* it is likely to be worst at what is thought of as the highest point. It seems obviously undesirable to put power of this kind into the hands of men. How does Père Congar describe this later period? What in his view has this combination of centralization and infallibility meant? He says nothing of the abuses to which this kind of absolute authority is subject (other chapters from the same book *Problems of Authority* do go into this subject) but simply describes it. He is standing at a moment when the authoritarian phase had reached its extreme, and almost certainly final point, and writing, before the opening of the Second Vatican Council, about the post-Tridentine period:[1]

'The Church reasserted her authority and not only her own, but the authority of God, of his Revelation (First Council of the Vatican), of Christ (Christ the King), of the State (encyclicals of Leo XIII), and the authority of parents. Ecclesiology, as far as the instruction of clerics and of the faithful is concerned, became fixed in a set pattern in which the question of authority is so predominant that the whole treatise is more like a hierarchiology or a treatise on public law. In this assertion of authority, the Papacy receives the lion's share. The idea of authority, the exercise of authority in contemporary Catholicism, are first and foremost the idea and the exercise of papal authority. The Pope is really *episcopus universalis*. Each individual Catholic has a much more immediate relationship with him than with his own bishop, as far as the general pattern of his Christian life is concerned. The encyclicals tell him what he ought to think, the liturgy is regulated by Roman documents, as are also fasting, canonical preparation for marriage, the *Ratio studiorum* of seminaries and the canonically erected faculties. The saints we venerate are those canonized

[1] *Op. cit.* pp. 144-5.

by Rome; religious congregations ask Rome for the authorization of their rule and it is from Rome that the secular Institutes have received theirs. Rome intervenes directly in the question of adapting apostolic methods to the needs of the times (worker priests, *Mission de France*). She keeps a sharp eye on publications, books, reviews, even catechisms, and, on occasion, orders their suppression. In short, the exercise of authority in the modern Catholic Church is largely that of its central and supreme seat in Rome.

'At a time when the modern world is attempting to build its life on the principle of the individual personality, even to the point of disregarding or denying the objective rights of God and of his law, the Catholic Church since the sixteenth century has put into practice a genuine "mystique" of authority in which the influence of the Society of Jesus has doubtless played its part. This "mystique" may be characterized as the notion of a complete identification of God's will with the institutional form of authority. In the latter, it is God himself whose voice we hear and heed. The fairly wide margin which the Middle Ages still left for the subordinate's appraisal is for all practical purposes, reduced almost to nothing. The Pope is the Visible Christ, "gentle Christ on earth" as St Catherine had already said. And every superior is to some extent the visible Christ. Some have even spoken of a real presence of Christ under the pontifical species. Further, the present period has seen, in France at least, a frequent and new use of the terms *Hierarchy* and *Magisterium*, which, at the level of terminology, indicate a healthy but very powerful insistence on authority.'

When we look at the historical influences of every kind which helped to create this tradition, the folly of it is somewhat softened. But the facts remain. The gospel has been transposed, to a great extent, into a rigid system. In a way it mirrors the system which the Jews had set up in Jerusalem. Catholic prelates appear precisely to be 'binding burdens on men's backs'; they and their systems seem to be something very like 'whitewashed mausolea'.

What then of the modern Catholic retreat from and criticism of all this, the *aggiornamento* as it is called, since Pope John XXIII inaugurated it? It was a Catholic, Lord Acton, who enunciated the modern variant of or sequence from *corruptio optimi pessima*: absolute power corrupts absolutely. We can trace the modern Catholic movement to this and other similar sources. And we can show that it gathered steadily increasing force until it had its totally unexpected climax in the reign of Pope John XXIII, and a subtle but firm support from Paul VI. But the objector may say: 'Too late! How can this change of heart be taken seriously after a thousand years and more of a bad tradition? Surely once Catholics found themselves in the majority again, and in power, they would soon erect a modern international equivalent of the Roman Curia and have all the world crawling to their measure, still certain that they were God's only real servants and had his special commission to rule the world, a sacred duty. Look at Spain. Look at Italy.' Within its limits there is strictly no answer to such an objection, with its projection of the past into the future. If an attempt is made to say that the Church never really identified herself with the bad ways and traditions, the answer is a flat contradiction. Whatever theory may say, the facts are clear: the Church was identified with and committed to these bad traditions and in part still is. To cap it, the objector can say that the *aggiornamento* has in any case not yet had the seal of success put on it; the conservatives still hold many, probably most, of the real points of power in the Church.

My brief is not only to state an objection but to answer it also. And the brief is just, for I myself am a Catholic; if the objection were for me unanswerable it would be difficult to remain a sincere and committed member of the Roman Catholic Church. What is it then which makes this objection not overwhelming? First, it may be well to make the small point that the Church does not claim that her members are sinless; a pope must make use of the sacrament of confession, like any other member of the Church—and like any other member of the Church he can abuse that sacrament if he wishes. There is no question of wishing to deny that many Catholics have been guilty of terrible evil. To the objection itself, the only answer, it seems, must be along the lines that the balance of charity, of goodness, of holiness, and the balance of achievement, holy, human and valuable, outweighs the bad. My case is that the historical picture as a whole enables us to say that the Church *is* a sacrament of the divine assistance, *is* the sacrament of God in a special way not to be found elsewhere on earth, that she does qualify as the inspiration of all men. The Catholic identifies the Church as 'one' and 'holy' and 'apostolic', according to the creeds of the early Church—a body of followers of Christ having special unity shown forth in their worship and their lives, having a special godliness, and having a sacramental continuity from the time of the first followers of Christ. If the case is to be made out we must find another and stronger tradition in the Catholic Church than that of triumphalism, a tradition more worthy, nearer to the gospels, and at all times active in the Church, one which though less showy has always played a primary part.

If we look at the heart of that era when the Church's legalist tradition was growing so fast, we can find a figure whose life was a living contradiction of legalism, and whose loyalty to and love of the Church was such that any attempt to put him outside her must be dismissed as unhistorical. St Francis became a myth. But the man St Francis was a Catholic, and totally loyal to the Roman See. He was a unique person, but he also symbolized and was in this sense typical of the spirit of personal charity, of love toward man and love toward God which, spread abroad in the lives of ordinary people and coming to a climax in the lives of the saints, was in fact a stronger and more significant tradition than that of the Church's rulers. If we want a witness to the understanding of this truth we might point to that of William Langland, the English author of *Piers Plowman*; Christ is the reality, the personal and sacramental daily reality for him, and this means the service of man by man and of love for fellow men if necessary to death. St Francis is important because he stands not only for the simplicity and detachment of a Christian life, but also for its involvement, its influence in politics and war, local and international, a disinterested purely Christian involvement. What can Père Congar say when he turns, after his depressing picture of authoritarianism rampant, to the other side of the coin?[1]

'Protests were made. We shall not cease to insist that one of these has never been taken seriously enough, either at the time or since, by the historiographers. I refer to the protest represented by the more or less anti-ecclesiastical spiritual movements so frequent in the twelfth century and which continued in the Franciscan spiritual movement down to the fourteenth

[1] *Op cit.* pp. 142–3.

century when it was succeeded by Lollardism and subsequently by the Hussite movement. All these movements, each from its own point of view and within its own terms of reference said the same thing: "Less pomp and more of the Gospel! You are Constantine's Church, not the Church of the Apostles." St Bernard who did battle with Arnold of Brescia, Henri de Lausanne and the neo-Manicheans did not scruple to repeat these explosive criticisms. He wrote to Eugenius III: "You allow yourself to be over-burdened with decisions you have to give in all kinds of external and secular cases. As far as you are concerned, I hear of nothing but awards and 'laws'. All this, as well as claims to prestige and riches, goes back to Constantine not to Peter."

'In a more general and perhaps more profound way, theology preserved many elements of the ancient ecclesiology, in a balanced view which lasted until the death of the two greatest thirteenth century doctors, Thomas and Bonaventure. In St Thomas, for instance, the idea of the Church as *Congregatio fidelium* is very much alive, and includes the theology of the return to God of man made in his image. Authority is not looked upon as a mere formal and juridical value; it is linked to the spiritual gifts, to the achievement of Christian perfection which is the perfection of charity, and so, by the same token, to the achievement of spiritual liberty and the gift of self in loving service. Matt. 16: 19 is interpreted as referring principally to Peter's confession of faith. The theology of the new law as formulated in the I^a–$II^{\text{æ}}$ qu. 106 and in the Scriptural commentaries, is completely Evangelical and certainly represents a fundamental category in St Thomas's ecclesiology.

'We should be guilty of a serious omission if we failed

to mention also what we might call the right of conscience. This principle was a vital force down to the Reformation, after which the condemnation of its abuse involved the end of its use. This is a vast field of research demanding special study. It includes, to begin with, the right of resistance to tyranny in the political sphere, and the right to enter religion or to change from one Order to another. It then deals with the protection of the poor and the weak—a traditional function of episcopal authority—and the notions of unjust excommunication, the right of protest, the right also to disobey *filialiter et obedienter* to quote from a letter of Robert Grosseteste to the Pope.'

We may add to this a word from Père Congar showing his view of the present main trend, which he clearly places in line with, or as the beginning of, the revival of the good tradition.[1]

'Priests are ceaselessly taken taken up with pastoral "cases", with a ministry of personal help and support, with repair and rescue work. But all of them, bishops and priests, have a very keen sense of their pastoral and apostolic responsibility. The adjective "apostolic" represents in itself a whole programme, it signifies a historical change in the application of the term "apostolic" which in modern times has come to mean zealous and having the missionary spirit. It cannot be denied that the exercise of authority in the Church today is marked by a predominance of pastoral care over prelacy, of tasks and responsibilities over the claiming of privileges.'

Perhaps the most fundamental point about this other tradition is that it is one of change—the Church is always

[1] *Op. cit.* pp. 147–8.

changing, because the Church is at the service of all, because she is intended by God as a community for all men and must therefore allow the modes of her life to be radically adapted at different places and times. The bad tradition is maintained precisely by those who have preached the abstract theory of the unchanging Church, the idea of the Church as the only steady point of reference in a changing and half-crazed world. Doctrinally this preaching has failed to make the distinction between on the one hand the unchanging facts of Jesus Christ, of his gospel and of the sacramental community he founded, and on the other the men who have the task of mediating knowledge and experience of these facts and administering the sacraments. Whilst the latter must have some kind of commission and must have the special protection of the Church yet they remain men and can err, and in any case have the historical task of being 'all things to all men'. The facts of the Church's history confirm that the Church, whilst holding to the unchanging gospel, has always been changing herself, according to the needs of different peoples, and according to the understanding of the gospel which different peoples can contribute to the Christian tradition; through these different peoples the Church has always been attempting a deeper and more precise understanding of Jesus Christ, and the Bible.

The Church has a feudal face because most of her institutions developed in a feudal society. The Church is now, with a vast and clamorous labour, changing its face. When we look at this, and at the theory of the changing, as distinct from unchanging, Church, and at the present manifest change, the objection begins to look much less cogent. The claim that the conservatives are in fact still in power can be countered. This essay is no place to attempt an assessment of the contest between the conservatives and the progressives. But a crucial point perhaps is the fact that lay consultation has been re-established sufficiently firmly for its spread throughout all sectors of the Church to be merely a matter of time. And it is a matter of profound interest that the crucial actions were taken in almost equal degrees by Popes Pius XI and XII. It was Pius XI who protected young Fr Cardijn from the Belgian Catholic *bien-pensants* and enabled him to found the *Jeunesse Ouvrière Chrétienne* (Pius XI, in time, will be seen to be a man of outstanding ability and courage, issuing his outright condemnations of both Fascism and of Communism, at a time when many other people and institutions were hesitating, not sure which way the cat might jump and lacking the ability to judge them). But it is Pius XII's action which might be taken as a symbol of that better tradition which has always been at work, even at times which in other ways may seem to be ultra-authoritarian. Pius XII kept too many things in his own hands, so it was said with great justification. He was an autocrat, in many ways. But some of his actions can be seen as sowing the seeds of that *aggiornamento* which would so quickly relegate his own reign to the status of that of the last of the era of autocracy and centralization.

It was Pius XII who called the First World Congress of the Lay Apostolate. To this concourse in 1951 came over 1,000 lay men and women, sent officially by the bishops of each country, to discuss virtually every problem facing the Church in the world. There was a Second Congress in 1957. The *Acta* of both congresses have been published in Rome. Other 'continental' congresses have been held. As a result a permanent office and a permanent Lay Council are now centred in Rome, and used for consultation by the Holy See. The national lay groups which sent representatives to the Congresses are gradually attaining the status of consultative groups. In

England and Wales this body, the National Council of
the Lay Apostolate, has been consulted by the Bishops
on the matter of the Nuclear Deterrent and the Oral
Contraceptive; through it a significant percentage of
practising Roman Catholics have had the opportunity
of stating their views on paper, and of being assured that
they would form the basis for a report to the bishops by
the National Council, in time for the third session of the
Second Vatican Council.

All this was begun by Pius XII, under the influence
of Mgr Cardijn. It is of a piece with the *volte-face* which
he inaugurated on the question of Church, State and
'toleration' in his speech to Italian Catholic Jurists in
December 1954. Since then this seed has grown into a
sizeable tree, despite the efforts of Curia and Holy
Office. The American Fr Courtney Murray, S.J., is
perhaps the priest most notably associated with this
development. Among the episcopate, Archbishop Denis
Hurley of Durban and Bishop de Smedt in Belgium have
been notable during and at the first two sessions of the
Vatican Council in developing the idea that the State
has no competence of any kind in religious affairs.
'The State has no religious obligations whatsoever
under the New Testament. The consequence of this
is that the Church cannot demand of the State,
even of a State representing a completely Catholic
society, that it use its political powers in favour of the
Church. To make such a demand is to ask the State to
act *ultra vires*.'[1]

The original traditions of early Church and gospel
are thus being redeployed to play a major role. These are
the traditions of a religious community, independent and
not seeking to exercise special political influence, a
religious community whose rules and regulations are

[1] Archbishop Hurley, *Herder Correspondence*, July, 1964.

intended to reflect the norms of the gospel, and to be reasonably flexible (as distinct from inflexibly canonical) as increasing understanding of the gospel is attained. It is impossible to provide total comfort for our objector. The bad traditions could, in theory, come to the top again. But to assess the objection justly it is necessary to decide whether or not the Church has survived and grown to its present status as a result of the good tradition or the bad tradition. It appears to me that it is the Saints, those like St Francis, and the vast number of other un-celebrated representatives of the great tradition who have in fact been at the heart of the Church's action, and that the Church has survived, generally, in spite of, rather than because of, the bad tradition of worldly influence and autocracy.

Our objection as stated in the first place was that the Church has institutionalized the gospel. Have we dealt fully with this? Even in the good tradition the Church remains for Catholics an institution. We may still feel the last word is said when we listen to Jesus's denunciation of the 'scribes and pharisees' and when we look with horrified fascination at the likeness of some of their ways with some of the ways of our prelates. But what is left of this objection after our previous argument is really a pseudo-objection. If the denunciation is simply personal, to those Pharisees, and these prelates, it is simply per-sonal, and is not part of our present objection. But if it is thought to be an objection to an institution as Institution then it cannot be maintained. Jesus was not denouncing the Law, or any Institution, but its abuse. He was a faithful Jew. The Chosen People as well as being a 'holy community' were a human society organized with its own proper rules. Christians from the start regarded their Church as a fulfilment of the promise which lay at the heart of this Jewish tradition. Roman Catholicism, along with the great majority of other Christian bodies, is sure that Jesus did not intend a purely 'charismatic' association of followers. Pharisaism is a very horrid thing; nothing more easily enrages a man than the stifling of love by law. But institutions are necessary. Without them life withers away in violence and chaos. Our objection was that institutionalism, legalism, autocracy, political influence, had become the whole life of the Church, that this was Catholicism, that this was the Catholic brand of Christianity. The objection was not to an institution as such, but to its abuse.

At the heart of the Catholic vision and of the Christian message lies the twofold idea of the absolute value of every individual person and the universality, for all men, all creation, all space, all time, of that Christian message. It seems to me that the Church herself is little more than an infant yet and that her venerable traditions may, due proportion being kept in this simile, be likened to the little ritual habits of an infant recently weaned. They have changed in the past and they are changing again now. The best of them show forth the love which is at the heart of the Christian gospel; the worst of them have failed to stifle that love.

Authoritarianism, Conformity and Guilt

FRANK ROBERTS

THE Catholic Church is an enigma for many. Her teaching seems to have the nature of an arcane discipline; her worship, conducted by a carefully, chosen and anointed priesthood, is redolent of mystery, with its precise ceremonial, its ancient liturgy, its melodies chanted in traditional modes, long since left behind in the onward development of European music. But apart from this worship, there is another aspect of Catholic religious life which seems to underline this historical remoteness and mystery. It is the authoritarian power which the Church exercises over its members.

In a world in which men tend to agree that Jack's opinion is as good as his master's, there is a further aspect of Catholicism which strikes people as incongruous, namely the Church's emphasis upon orthodoxy. To pronounce belief in a creed, to accept a fixed form of utterance put into one's mouth, seems out of place to people outside the Catholic tradition of Christianity. Protestants see the believer as one who answers for himself, one to whom is extended liberty of individual interpretation. What is looked for in a fellow-Protestant is the acceptance of a common Christian attitude to life rather than a common assent to Christian dogmas. To Protestants or the simply uncommitted, Catholicism seems to be a way of life in which assent and obedience are valued more than understanding and consent.

To the outsider, for example, many Catholics would appear to be more preoccupied with keeping the letter of the law than the spirit. And if there is any doubt about this, let an individual Catholic consider what sins will bring him to confession. Eating meat on Fridays and missing Sunday Mass? But what about the sins of uncharity? Sarcasm towards one's fellow-men; the repetition of unproven gossip; refusal to give alms to a needy cause; supporting an unjust wage-claim by one's trade union; or the claims of one's profession to an unwarrantably high fee; or of one's business association to an unduly high margin of profit? The argument is not that such faults may go unconfessed, but whether Catholics consider these to be sins barring them from Communion in the way that the rule-breaking faults do.

There are certain social reforms of the last 150 years which contemporary society, looking back upon, can scarcely regard as reversible. The wrongness of slavery; the abuse of child labour and the iniquity of terms of employment that allowed no say to employees—all such reforms mark an advance away from that kind of social structure in which human beings in one group could exploit the dependence of those in another group. Many will ask what part the Church played in initiating these

social changes. How can we account for this con-
ventionalism and legalism in religious observance?
Perhaps we should look to childhood for it. Maybe that
in-so-far as the child is the father of the man, so in child
psychology we can find a clue to adult piety. Students of
the psychology of childhood note that there is a period in
a child's moral development called 'moral realism'. It is
an attitude to conduct and behaviour at its strongest at
about six years old. This realism has a certain point of
view which is characterized by three features:

(a) Duties are regarded as externally imposed and
the goodness of acts lies in their expressing obedience
to rules. Bad acts are bad because they do not conform
to rules.

(b) The letter of the law is of prior obligation.

(c) Acts are valued not by their intention, but
rather by their conformity to external rules.

This is a way of looking at life which is artless and
naive. When one considers the age when children are
observed to be thinking like this, the whole ingenuous
simplicity is easily understood. But it is not long after
this age, namely at about seven, that children are
prepared for their first Communion and are, being now
at the 'age of reason', considered fit to begin to live by the
Sacraments. They are prepared first in terms of the rules
which characterize the pattern of adult religious observance. What are to be their obligations as full members of
their church. What are they told? Be sure never to miss
Sunday Mass. Go regularly to Holy Communion.
Prepare well for receiving the Sacrament; and what
better preparation than self-examination and confession?
Keep the holidays of obligation. Avoid mortal sin. The
time, the *very* time, when most Catholic children are
being given these injunctions, is that time of life when

already they tend to see the rules of conduct as having an external validity in their own right. And it is just when they are conceiving of regulations as having that quality of transcendental immutability, that the whole of this attitude gets maximum reinforcement, at the time of first Communion.

It seems very probable that the emotional highlighting of the occasion of first Communion at this age serves to fixate in children a rule-keeping attitude to religion which persists into later life. Perhaps this firm and uncomplicated presentation of their religion will serve best for many of them. Yet is it wise that there should be imposed upon them a childish attitude to religious behaviour at a time when it is all too easy to fixate them into a pattern of pietist obedience which may persist into adult years?

Another point of child-psychology is the question of children's notions of the sanctions of morality. A child has learnt at his first Communion to use the Sacrament of Confession as a means of correction. We may suppose that after a few years of trying to be good, he begins to have some awareness of the limitations of his ability to avoid sin. And what will be his ideas of the likely penalties for failure? In one of Piaget's studies of children's ideas of what constitutes a suitable punishment for misdeeds, an important trend is noted. From the age of six years until twelve, the idea that the true nature of punishment is that of retaliation grows year by year. It is noteworthy because these are the years during which the child is learning the difficulties of dealing with sins. Now, too, he learns, for good or ill, that the penalty for mortal sin is the ultimate one: eternal punishment. May it not be that the spiritual experiences of these years, seen in terms of God 'paying one back' for sin, will characterize the young Catholic's religion for the rest of his life? It is not unlikely that many a Catholic, having been thus started off in the practice of his religion, will, under difficulty or strain, regress to just that attitude in his relationship to God which is more appropriate to childhood than to adult years—a reaction least suited to any spiritual crisis. This negative kind of self-preoccupation with formulae for conduct hinders the development of the kind of Christianity which trains men to be a leaven in society. Members of the clergy themselves have pointed to the weakness of religion of this type. But it continues to persist, encouraged by so many priests who are trained to believe that such docility is commendable. Such was the viewpoint of a priest recently appointed to a very large parish in the New World. Asked what his new parishioners were like, he declared, 'Wonderful, wonderful. They will do anything I want.' Was it not the legalism of Jewish piety which Our Lord censured in calling his followers to a quality of justice that exceeded that of the Scribes and Pharisees? What de Greef calls a 'defence personality' tends in some Catholics, perhaps the majority of those most faithful to religious practice, to become the typical pattern. It is a pattern, moreover, which is characteristic of an immature psychological growth. Should not the crises of religious commitment in children be delayed until they come to more adult ways of thought and behaviour? Should not Communion, Confession and Confirmation come after the eleventh birthday, rather than before?

Many child psychologists have shown that after about eleven reasoning powers develop in children and are brought sharply to bear upon all aspects of life around them. Piaget in particular has shown how children at that age are no longer bound to the concrete illustration, but are capable of deeper and more abstract thinking. This, surely, is the age at which children should have

77

their religion presented to them as an aid to emancipation from childish thinking. As was suggested by the Medico-Social and Psycho-Pedagogic Commission of the International Catholic Child Bureau,[1] 'from a truly Christian standpoint, religious training is synonymous with progressive liberation'. An acceptance of one's responsibility for religious beliefs should surely come as children attain adult mentality. Parents and teachers and all who have to do with children's religious formation need to be aware of the scale of values they impose upon children's minds. Of course a child must learn to love good and renounce evil, to choose the right and avoid wrong-doing. But children are very ready to adopt adults' moral injunctions whilst still very young, thus conditioning themselves to harsh judgements of each other and themselves. They are easily made to feel guilty and anxious, and such reactions are readily brought out quite late in their childhood.

'Where prohibitions of natural impulses are allied to religious sanctions in a harsh and joyless way, a strongly pervasive feeling of guilt may be built in the child's mind from which he can never free himself, or only by a complete denial of faith.'[2]

The point for adults to bear in mind is that the oppression of a child's conscience contributes little to its moral formation. As Flugel puts it, 'Feelings of inferiority (the psycho-analysts) admit are genuine and frequent, but . . . play a lesser role in the determination of moral goods, attitudes or conduct. Such feelings are . . . more likely to be the consequence than the cause of moral ideals.'[3]

[1] W. D. Wall, *Education and Mental Health*, p. 151, UNESCO, Paris, 1955.
[2] Ibid., p. 101.
[3] J. C. Flugel, *Man, Morals and Society*, p. 59, Pelican Books.

These considerations are of equal importance for those who teach in Catholic schools as for parents. Even in the Catholic community, parents tend to leave to teachers the religious education of their children. Yet parents need to take a larger share in training the children in religion, in order to avoid the inevitable attitude of regarding 'R.I.' as just another school subject. Moreover, some teachers tend to put themselves not only 'in loco parentis' with respect to their pupils but also 'in loco sacerdotis', tending to take over an authoritarian role. How many still quiz their pupils about attendance at Sunday Mass and Communion?

A child's main religious development for life occurs during school-days. Whilst conscientious teachers take care with their pupils, it seems that in many of our schools corporal punishment still exists—more perhaps than in non-Catholic ones. In English Catholic public schools this tradition is still firmly entrenched. They should study the Quaker educational tradition as exemplified by Mr. Kenneth Barnes of Wennington School, York. Psychological studies of the learning process are said to be notoriously weak in relation to education, but one finding does hold and this is that, in comparison with reward, the effect of punishment is minimal in effecting learning.

Another question—What is the place of guilt in a Catholic's spiritual life, and how is it to be assessed? Perhaps the most straightforward way is to consider the concrete instance. John Smith, a Catholic, whom we observe leaving a church one Saturday evening, has been to Confession. For some months he has absented himself from the Sacraments. What has kept him away has been his own deliberate choice. He has done something which his church calls mortal sin. At first the matter of mortal sin had not much vexed him but before long he began to feel a disquiet. His family continues the practice of their religion and he feels isolated from them: increasingly he feels, too, the growth of 'distance' between himself and God. Presently remorse catches up with him. A sense of guilt deriving from his shame takes hold of him. Soon he finds his way to church and the confessional.

In John Smith's case we recognize a condition of self-censure, leading to his seeking forgiveness. This is what theologians are talking about when they discuss guilt. Wherein, however, does the fact of guilt lie? Theological guilt is a state of knowledge. The wrongdoer knowingly has done wrong and is aware that he has transgressed the law of God. The guilt exists in the fact of knowing. The act is considered and conscious self-judgement is made. But in John Smith's story there is more than the act of self-judgement and the knowledge of wrong-doing. Not only has he made the self-accusation in confession, but something has led up to this. Even before the confession was made, the self-judgement involved in theological guilt had already been made; but, still more, this had been accompanied by specific feelings: of remorse, of shame at his isolation from God and from his family.

Here we have not simply an act, nor only a judgement. Here is an experienced state, and one which is proper to the situation. The feeling is typical as a normal, even healthy, emotional reaction. Not only was what was done seen to be wrong, it was felt to be wrong. Now it may well be considered that this emotional concomitant, this *feeling*, is unnecessary to theological guilt. We might say that in-so-far as the fault is recognized and the sin acknowledged, no accompanying feelings are needed to validate the fact of guilt. But this surely is not all we mean by guilt? Consider a parallel situation which shows up the cold intellectualism of such a viewpoint. There is a kind of mental abnormality, half-delinquency, called the psychopathic state. A psychopath has virtually no conscience. Because he lacks those feelings for his fellow men which constitute the bonds of social solidarity, the psychopath can seek his own ends without reference to the good or ill of others. Whilst he may well *know* that it is wrong to beat up an old woman and rob her, yet he does not *feel* it is wrong. Presumably that he should *know* is of prior importance, but it is the fact of his being unable to *feel* the wrongness of his deed that is the critical fact of his abnormal condition. The guilt of a sinner may well lie in his acknowledgement of culpability, but for most of us the guilt without the feeling, the knowledge without the sense of wrong, would scarcely seem to be guilt at all.

Where something evil has been done, the mind at once recognizes that society can call upon the wrong-doer to acknowledge responsibility, and with the knowledge that one is the wrong-doer the feeling of responsibility to society and to God becomes overwhelming. This is where the concomitant feeling gives meaning to that act of self-judgement of which theological guilt consists.

Here we are at the borderland of psychology and morals. The overlap is inevitable. For many psychologists, discussion of moral values is only possible in the 'objective' field of motivational and attitude studies.

In a discussion,[1] Grey Walter mentions the fact that the sense of responsibility is associated with feelings of guilt, and this sense must seemingly play a part in normal social development. He goes on to point out the lack of this sense in delinquents. 'They don't consider that freedom of action implies responsibility for action.' The

[1] *Discussions on Child Development*, Vol. III, Tavistock Publications, London, 1958.

nature of real guilt then is, first, that it should be recog- nized, secondly, that the sense of one's responsibility should evoke an acknowledgement of one's errors, and thirdly, there should be a feeling of guilt. This last feature, objectively speaking, is of the least importance, but in the subject himself the lack of feelings of guilt would be a serious matter. In the case of a psychopath, his lack of feeling is an index of his pathological state. Besides the normal state of guilt, which is recognizable by these three features, a state of neurotic guilt is recognized. This is the condition which is, truly, morbid. A person so affected may not only feel a sense of guilt but also a sense of responsibility, as for a wrong act. The difference between the real thing and the false is clear, and it lies in the objective *fact* of responsibility in the former and the lack of it in the latter. The feeling then can be absent in the case of the truly guilty and can be present in the case of the actually innocent; either condition being itself pathological. Consider now a condition of pathological guilt. The case chosen is factual. J. is the daughter of parents married late in life. From infancy her mother's rejection of J. has been pro- nounced, but not to a point of material neglect. Food, clothing and continuous home care have been provided in a well-to-do household. J. saw little of her father but when he did appear at home, she received from him the few crumbs of parental interest she ever got. Clearly he did not reject her, but equally clearly he was unwilling to spend with her more than a few odds and ends of his spare time. These, however, were valued the more since her mother's rejection continued. As J. progressed through adolescence these times with her father grew fewer. His business took him further afield. J.'s jealousy of her father's business interests grew as her time with him decreased. She became resentful of his meanness, and in an outburst of anger wished him dead. A few days later the father, returning home from an overseas business occasion, was killed in a plane crash.

J.'s subsequent history is one of serious mental illness. The dramatic nature of her father's death was not the cause of her illness, but it gave a clear direction to its nature, for an anxiety state with severe phobias and guilt for her father's death characterized her illness. Her outburst in which she voiced a death wish on her father was too close to his violent demise not to have appeared to be the cause of it. Here again is a symptom which owes something to fixation at an infantile level of reasoning. For almost any children at some time in their lives the oddest sequences of events are seen as cause and effect. Stories are manifold of the way this works. For example, a small boy yields to temptation and steals some change from his mother's purse. That night he is awakened by a heavy summer thunderstorm. What is this latter but the retributory act of Fate about to exact due penalty for his wrong-doing?

As children grow up they tend to outgrow such un-fruitful modes of thinking. But in the person who is prone to neurotic guilt, whether of so grave a kind as to require hospitalization, or of the less serious kind, we are dealing with a state of arrested psychological develop-ment. An infantile view of cause and effect is retained. So in neurotic guilt responsibility may be asserted for non-existent crimes. In other cases free-floating anxiety may well up in the neurotic, expressing itself in a sense of guilt by fastening upon an event in this way.

Similar to this are the scruples of the penitent who, having been to Confession, is oppressed by the thought that some fault may not have been confessed or that some aspect of a deed done may not have been seen in the guilty light which reveals the true nature of the penitent.

Such over-scrupulosity can reach a degree of exaggeration which approaches a pathological condition.

Fortunately this kind of guilt is readily recognized by priests. Few of them will be slow to deal promptly and prudently with guilt of this pathological nature. Non-Catholics, critical of the practising Catholic's attitude to Confession, may well be surprised to learn that in cases of this kind where excessive scrupulosity is manifest, a penitent may be strictly enjoined to *refrain* from Confession. The Church's regulation of her sacrament requires an intelligent participation. The opposite of compulsion by the Church is brought to bear in the case of morbid guilt. Confession, a vehicle for true penitence and genuine repentance, does not commonly operate as an occasion for the propagation of neurotic guilt.

The Catholic's sense of guilt is at times seen as the means by which the clergy are able to wield their authority over the laity. The guilt of the penitent brings him to the confessional, there to receive penance and advice for his correction. The system depends upon the perpetuation of feelings of guilt for wrong-doing. To what extent is there some perpetuation of a sense of guilt in pastor as well as penitent? This is a question which would not be regarded as senseless by those who (in the parent-child relationship which we shall consider later), see a perpetuation of the parental sense of guilt in a child's religious upbringing as a Catholic. Clearly, if there is such a sense of guilt it can scarcely be the result of responsible religious development. If it derives from priests, then it is likely to derive from their defects of personality, or their lack of the right sense of vocation.

When considering the nature of Catholic religious vocation, some non-Catholics hold that celibacy is too exacting a way of life. But when the nature of a vocation is clearly seen and consciously and deliberately entered upon, there is less danger. The harm comes when there is no willing offering of oneself to fill a need, but only the oppression of constraint. For constraint which is due to some external cause, such as entering upon a vocation to satisfy a parent's ambition, or a sense of duty to family, has only one parallel, itself equally harmful, surely, and that is the inner compulsion arising from some unknown and unreasoning sense of sheer obligation which will not be gainsaid. Are some 'vocations' of this latter type?

How then should a vocation come about in terms of the psychology of the process? If some vocations are inadequate, we may ask, 'Was the manner of their formation psychologically sound and healthy?' Perhaps a comparison may wisely be made betweeen a vocation which follows the Self-Ideal, and one which is a product of the Super-Ego. The earliest beginnings of the formation of the Self-Ideal will take place in the infant's emotional life during the course of its reactions to its family circle. From the start the child learns to love and admire parents for having what it does not have: an amazing control of themselves and the world; the ability to love, giving without fear of loss; the readiness to spend time and concern not about themselves but about the infant. These good qualities are something the child lacks. Parental power in this respect is tremendous in contrast to the child's weak powers.

That the child lacks these things because of its immaturity does not occur to it; the possession of these powers of goodness is itself a virtue. The child makes an intuitive appraisal of the good in its parents. The appraisal has both an intellectual and an emotional side. The child sees in the parents what it wants to be like, and comes to admire, to respond with this emotion to the ideal. Intellectually, it sees as worthwhile the goodness of the parents. Intellectually, too, it perceives all too

clearly the wide difference between the powerful goodness of the parents and its own lack and weakness. This
sense of weakness induces imitative action. The child
wants to be like the admired ones, and copies their
actions: they become its models.

This is a process which is taking place recurrently
throughout early childhood until, with the widening of
the social *milieu*, perceptions, appraisals and these self-
identifying imitations are extended to other admired
figures. The model of the admired good in parents
provides the pattern of integration into society at large.
This is perhaps the human analogue of that process in
certain social animals called imprinting, where the infant
creature, through an instinctively learnt following
response, becomes attached to the elders of its own
species. The occurrence of this process seems critical to
the successful integration of the individual into the society
of its species, since, failing its occurrence during these
earliest years, even the animal's ability to mate at maturity
appears to be impaired. So through its parents the infant
child is emotionally bound to them, yet the process of
appraisal by which this occurs in children goes beyond
the merely emotional and includes the intellectual.

Going beyond this procedure, however, we come to a
concept by which the growing child is discovering not
merely the general context of its relation to society, but
the individual index of what it is to become within that
society. Here is something like Adler's 'guiding fiction',
as well as like Freud's Ego-Ideal. The Self-Ideal, however, is closely associated with the moral factor. It is the
seeing in one's ideal self those qualities one has learnt.
By contrast with this, consider the operation of the Super-
Ego. This is a censor and a check on the ego or self which
has grown up through the years. All moral judgements,
all ethical standards for the assessment of conduct, one's

own especially, become internalized during childhood as they are taken over from one's elders, especially of course the parents. Its parents' evaluation of what is good and what is evil, its teachers' condemnations, its pastors' vetoes become internalized, so that in due course they are part of the process by which the child learns to control its own behaviour in terms of the injunctions and taboos which society has imposed. Clearly, the Super-Ego is much the same as conscience. But there are also respects in which it is not identifiable with the rational conscience of an informed Christian, for the Super-Ego retains something of the attitude characteristic of that time of life in which its foundations were laid down; it is infantile. Its strictures are, in fact, harsher than those of society. Its taboos are such as parents would not uphold. Lacking mercy, its condemnations exceed the standards of judgement of those from whom they were derived. The force and power of the Super-Ego derives from its ability to release aggression from the libidinous, the deeper, instinctive side of man's nature. One of Freud's disciples, Alexander, spoke of an 'alliance' between the *id*, the source of man's 'fleshly' demands, and the Super-Ego. By a transaction between these two sides of our nature, operating at the level of the unconscious, the Super-Ego could claim the right to exact punishment and impose suffering in return for concessions granted to the clamourous demands of the instinctive side of our nature. The two could thus 'gang up' upon the self. The Super-Ego, it follows, although in some respects like the Christian concept of conscience, is much harsher and more censorious.

Imagine now a vocation adopted in terms of the Super-Ego's force. Perhaps by way of an estrangement from parents, a young man incurs at an unconscious level a sense of guilt. Such a vocation is accepted in terms of self-punishment. The 'oughtness' of the response to a call to live a life of self-sacrifice is accepted in terms of remorse and reparation. The negative aspect of the moral obligation is stressed throughout. Here is little opportunity for the Ego to exercise reason, to weigh and consider. The choice is not one positively made, but rather an acceptance of the inevitable. Here is the infantile quality of the Super-Ego's operation.

A young man entering a seminary on these terms, or a young woman finding her way through to the religious life with this kind of 'conscience' as the dominant motive, may well be up against the impossible. What human being can sustain such motivation for years on end? It must be transformed, so that, from being impelled through a bald sense of obligation to fulfil one's destiny, one instead chooses, accepts and embraces such a way of life positively. Otherwise the intolerable nature of the burden is rejected, and the life is either abandoned, or is settled into in purely material terms, and its attendant duties mechanically performed. The 'Super-Ego vocation' is the one that must be suspect. It is the internal parallel of an externally enforced entry upon the ministry. Such kinds of enforcement, lacking the co-operation of a free-will, might make for unhappiness for years. Instances of this kind are rarer than once they used to be. An example which occurred in this century was of a devout actress, who nevertheless had an illegitimate child. Both the actress and her mother decided to make 'reparation' by training the boy to the priesthood. Such a notion of vocation, deriving from so unjustified a sense of obligation, lacks all reality.

In contrast to the 'compulsive' vocation, whether it arises in response to some external force, or more commonly, from a 'Super-Ego' driven response, how much better is the 'self-ideal' vocation, in which a man sees the realization of his highest desires, hopes and aspirations in the ministry of the Church. Consider the following of such a vocation, in which a man sees the realization of his highest desires, hopes and aspirations in the ministry of the Church. Consider the following of a vocation pursued in terms of the self-ideal.

With some diffidence an attempt has been made in this article to indicate one or two of the psychological factors that may well have been at work to induce that indifferent, conformist piety which many Catholics appear to show, and which in the contemporary world seems to be contributing so little to human enlightenment and the Christian redemption of society.

My conclusion would be that a wider place must be found in society for the active Catholic layman. He will have to make that place for himself. Not only has he to meet the humanists' recurrent charge of obscurantism—at times he will not even receive support from his own clergy. But if such men and woman are going to succeed in carrying conviction in the face of objections to Roman Catholicism which have some claim to be well-founded psychologically, then they must show a spirituality that is based not on a naive and unthinking orthodoxy, nor upon an uncritical acclamation of doctrinal uniformity, nor especially on fixation at an infantile level of timid docility, in other words self preoccupied with apprehensions about guilt, rules and conformity, but rather upon an apostolicity which is active, informed and responsible. In terms of the tactics and logistics of the Church's campaign in the present-day world such men will set the pace. They will do the thinking that lies behind the strategy. They will be a vanguard engaged in contest. And they will do all this in terms of a truly spiritual and sacramental support on the part of an enlightened and understanding clergy.

Censorship

PROFESSOR H. P. R. FINBERG

IN these days of universal literacy, when new universities are springing up like mushrooms, no authority
can expect to pass unquestioned, least of all, perhaps, one
which claims the right to impose restrictions on the free
exchange of ideas. Many who accept or can imagine
themselves accepting the religious and moral teaching of
the Catholic Church boggle at her system of censorship.
Always unpopular with those outside the fold, that
system has lately been attacked from within by churchmen as well as laymen, and there is now a very general
expectation that it will not emerge unaltered from the
process of self-examination and renewal undertaken by
the Church in her resolve to meet the challenge of the
modern world.

In its present form ecclesiastical censorship dates from
the sixteenth century. It was part of the Church's response

to the invention of printing. So long as books continued to be copied slowly and painfully by hand, editions could not be large. If a book was pronounced, for whatever reason, damnable, no important economic interest suffered when a ban was put on the making of further copies, and existing copies could without much trouble be rounded up, confiscated, and burnt. This procedure had at least the merit of a certain crude efficiency. But the multiplication of copies rendered possible by the new invention altered the picture. On the one hand, the printing press offered the Church a useful administrative tool and a powerful channel of propaganda; on the other, its use in enemy hands presented a challenge to which the Church as well as the State reacted vigorously. Hence a corpus of legislation, much of which remains in force to the present day.

The Code of Canon Law prescribes that no Catholic shall publish any work of theology, church history, ethics, or any other subject directly touching religion and morals, without first submitting it to ecclesiastical censorship. The publisher has some latitude: he need not go to his own bishop. He can seek a licence to print from the bishop of the diocese in which the author lives, or from the bishop in whose territory—it may be in a foreign country—the book is printed; and the choice is occasionally governed by a belief that one authority will be more sympathetic than another, but if the licence is refused by one he must disclose the fact when seeking it elsewhere.

Every diocese is supposed to have its own official for dealing with matters of censorship. As a rule he does not read the book himself, but passes it to a reader, always a man in holy orders, whom he believes to be particularly competent in the subject-matter. The book may be still in manuscript or typescript; some offices, however, insist quite arbitrarily on having printer's proofs. This is naturally more convenient for the reader, but it adds to the cost of any corrections which have to be made, or to the publisher's loss in the extreme case of a licence being refused. The reader's name is never divulged. He is enjoined to bring a strictly impartial mind to the task, dismissing all considerations which do not arise directly from the recognized teaching of the Church. Not all readers achieve this degree of objectivity. In that large area which is not covered by the Church's formal definitions there is plenty of room for divergent views, and sometimes a reader will suggest modifications to bring the text into accord with his personal opinions. It takes a strong-minded author to reject proposals conveyed to him from a quarter which is not the less authoritative for being anonymous. On the other hand, some authors willingly admit that they have profited by expert criticisms tendered through this channel. There may be more than one such exchange before the reader sends in his final report. If that is favourable, the diocesan official certifies his superiors that there is no obstacle ('nihil obstat') to the publication, and the bishop or his vicar-general then grants an imprimatur, or licence to print.

The rule laid down by Leo XIII in 1897, that no payment may be exacted for the censoring of books, is not now observed. A fee is charged commensurate in each case with the magnitude and difficulty of the task, the amount being fixed by the diocesan official. It is paid by the publishers, and is usually a very modest sum, too small to affect the price of the book.

A diocesan imprimatur carries with it no kind of guarantee. A book which has emerged without scathe from the preliminary test may yet be attacked after publication. If some reader considers that after all it offends in one or more respects against faith or morals, he may in the purity of his zeal—and it would be pleasant to believe that the step has never been taken from lower motives—lodge a complaint with a higher authority, the Supreme Congregation of the Holy Office, seated in Rome, and directed by a Cardinal Secretary under the personal presidency of the Pope.

The papacy has always asserted its competence to take direct action in matters of this kind. In 1520, to look no further back, Leo X ordered that all Lutheran books should be sought out and burnt, and in the following year he wrote to thank Cardinal Wolsey for the zeal he had shown in carrying out this decree. In 1564 the Council of Trent issued a comprehensive list of banned books, and soon afterwards a regular administrative machine of censorship was established by Pius V. Since then a large number of books have been condemned at Rome. Their titles, with the names of the authors and the date of the condemnatory decree, are printed in the Index of Prohibited Books, a volume which takes high rank among the curiosities of literature.

The Index has gone through several editions, of which the latest was published in 1948. It would be instructive to go through them noting which titles have been removed and which added in successive editions. It would also be an interesting statistical exercise to classify the condemned books by nationality of origin. Catholic Spain contributes relatively few, but then Spain was taken care of by its own Inquisition. The Poles have perhaps been too busy fighting or conspiring against their non-Catholic neighbours to invite repression in the realm of ideas. France, on the other hand, so long known as the eldest daughter of the Church, has always been prolific of ideas, and special pains have been taken to guard her from corruption. All the works of Zola,

Maeterlinck, and Anatole France are on the Index, with all the romances ('fabulae amatoriae') of Balzac, Stendhal, Sand, Sue, Dumas *père* and *fils*, and Murger. There too are *Madame Bovary*, *Salammbo*, *Notre Dame de Paris*, and *Les Misérables*. The jesters keep them company: Voltaire, of course, and La Fontaine's *Contes et Nouvelles*. By contrast, English literature comes off lightly, though Taine's *Histoire de la Littérature Anglaise* was condemned two years after publication. Sterne's *Sentimental Journey* is banned, but not his *Tristram Shandy*; and the subtitle *Virtue Rewarded* has not procured immunity for Richardson's *Pamela*.

True to its name, the Index is arranged in alphabetical order. Thus masterpieces which are household names figure side by side with the lucubrations of obscure and long-forgotten pamphleteers. At times one could imagine oneself to be looking through the stock-list of a bankrupt bookseller. The operations of the Holy Office are not strictly confined to the sphere of faith and morals. In the Code of Canon Law church history is expressly named as one of the subjects requiring censorship; and this means that the censors may at any time be called upon to pronounce on questions of historical accuracy. Since absolute power tends to corrupt absolutely, there must sometimes be a temptation to condemn historical or other writings not because they have been convicted of falsehood at any point, but simply because they report unwelcome truths. Not all censors agree with Pope Gregory the Great that 'if scandal is taken at the truth, it is better to let scandal arise than to abandon the truth'. Some books have come under the ban on the ground—though not, I believe, on the sole ground— that they are 'offensive to pious ears', and the ears of the pious are sometimes of asinine length.

John Stuart Mill, as we have been told in imperishable

95

verse, 'by a mighty effort of will, overcame his natural bonhomie and wrote *Principles of Political Economy*'. The Roman authorities are not lacking in bonhomie, but for all that they put him on the Index, where he figures in company with the historians, Burnet, Gibbon, Hallam, and the philosophers, Bacon, Berkeley, Bergson, Comte, Croce, Descartes, Hobbes, Hume, Montesquieu, Kant, Locke, Rousseau, and Spinoza. Whether or not one accepts the principles of censorship, it is at least intelligible that the writings of the powerful thinkers should have been considered dangerous; but one would suppose that a Latin work printed in London in 1665, prognosticating the final destruction of Rome in the following year, had by this time lost its power to alarm, and only actual perusal could reveal what perils lurk in an Italian treatise condemned in 1817, the work of 'a sub-alpine philanthropist', as he styles himself, on the Art of Preserving and Increasing the Beauty of Ladies.

It is possible to obtain leave to read any prohibited book for purposes of serious study. Failing such permission, to read knowingly ('scienter') a book which has been condemned by name is to incur the severest penalty the Church can inflict, an excommunication from which only the Holy See can absolve. There is much virtue in that 'scienter'. Few Catholics have ever seen the Index or would know where to find a copy if they wanted one. Just as Molière's bourgeois found that he had been talking prose without knowing it, so many educated Catholics must have read one or more of these prohibited works without being aware of either the prohibition or the spiritual danger. Others, perhaps, have cultivated a prudent ignorance.

There are, however, general prohibitions of a much wider range. The Code of Canon Law defines twelve categories of books which require no specific condemnation to remove them from a good Catholic's reading list. All obscene literature and all books deliberately aimed at subverting the Christian faith are prohibited *ipso facto*. Presumably their reputation is to convict them: how else can the faithful know them for what they are? The Code, wiser in this than our civil law, makes no attempt to define obscenity. There are passages in the Bible and in the Greek and Latin classics which would fall under almost any definition that could be framed. Generations of schoolboys, indeed, have been introduced to the facts of sexual life through 'the decent obscurity of a learned tongue', and many a seminarian has first learnt of certain vices from handbooks of moral theology. Yet the Church has no objection to Bible-reading in approved editions of the sacred texts, which do not require expurgation to secure approval, and the ancient classics are expressly excepted from the general condemnation of lascivious books, so highly is classical scholarship esteemed at Rome.

Anybody can denounce a published work to the central authority, secure in the knowledge that his identity will not be revealed. All the operations of the Holy Office, indeed, are shrouded in impenetrable secrecy. The criteria by which it judges are known only to itself. The author has no inkling that his book has been denounced, and is given no opportunity to defend it. Not without reason has the Holy Office been described as the most arbitrary tribunal in the civilized world.

From time to time the curtain is wrenched aside and daylight penetrates into the tenebrosities of this modern inquisition. It did so very notably in 1938, when readers of the *Times* were suddenly informed, by a letter from Lord Charnwood, of some remarkable facts concerning a book by the well-known poet and critic Alfred Noyes.

Noyes, a convert to Catholicism, had spent three

years preparing a detailed study of the life and writings of Voltaire. The book, which ran to more than 600 pages, was an elaborate and well-argued apologia for one who has been conventionally regarded as an arch-enemy of the Christian faith. In the ardour of his championship Noyes even convinced himself that Voltaire's relations with some of the women in his life, including Madame Denis, were never more than platonic. With greater force he argued that Voltaire was a sincere moralist, a theist, and fundamentally a better Christian than many of the churchmen he encountered in eighteenth-century France. This thesis he supported with ample quotations from Voltaire's published works and private correspondence.

The book was published in September 1936 by Sheed and Ward, the well-known Catholic house. It carried no imprimatur, the publishers having considered that it fell outside the categories of books for which a licence is required, and it does not appear that they were ever held to have erred in this respect. The first intimation of trouble came in May 1938, when the Cardinal Secretary of the Holy Office wrote to the Archbishop of Westminster, Cardinal Hinsley, informing him that the book has been denounced and that the Holy Office, after examining it, found it worthy of condemnation. The letter did not explain why or wherein it was held to be at fault. Thereupon Cardinal Hinsley, though considerably taken aback, informed the publishers and asked them to inform the author. The Holy Office had not as yet actually condemned the book, but they required it to be withdrawn from circulation, and Sheed and Ward were to be 'severely warned' for having published it.

Between the founding of the firm in 1926 and the receipt of this communication from the Holy Office Sheed and Ward had published a great many books of high quality without any visible encouragement from Rome. The *brutum fulmen* of May 1938 seems to have been the first sign that Rome knew of the firm's existence. But an open clash with the Church's central authority was something no Catholic publisher could afford; it might easily have been fatal to his business. Mr Sheed felt that he had no option but to suppress a new edition of the book which was ready and to withdraw from sale a large American edition. A French translation, not yet printed, was also put into cold storage. That these steps would involve author, publisher, and translator in appreciable pecuniary loss went for nothing with those who dealt the blow. What is money—especially other people's money—when the good of souls is at stake?

The Holy Office had also demanded that the author should write something equivalent to a reparation. A preposterous demand, as Noyes and his friends were not slow to point out, since he had been given no idea of the grounds on which exception was taken to his *Voltaire*. The decree wiped out three years of work, done in all good faith, but offered no explanation and allowed him not a word in his own defence. An added source of bitterness was the knowledge that, if he had given his book to a non-Catholic publisher, intimidation from Rome would have been of no avail, and *Voltaire* would have continued to circulate, at least until the author saw reason to modify or withdraw it. The technique employed by the Holy Office on this occasion was in fact the technique of blackmail. Noyes did not use that ugly word, but he protested that 'the free will and conscience of the author were completely swept aside . . . To submit would be against the law of religion and the church. With all due respect to the authorities, therefore, it is on this law that I must take my final stand.'

Had the book been submitted to ecclesiastical censorship before publication, and had an imprimatur then been refused, the author could have asked for an explanation, and would almost certainly have got it. Canon 1394 of the Code, based on a decree of 1898, provides that in such a case the reasons shall be indicated to the author on request, 'unless some grave cause require otherwise'. In defying the Holy Office, Noyes was insisting on his right to be treated as a being with a mind and conscience of his own. But he might have insisted in vain if the affair had remained secret. To prevent this, he told his non-Catholic friends what had happened. On August 10 the full iniquity of the procedure was revealed in Lord Charnwood's letter to the *Times*.

On the following day Cardinal Hinsley put himself on record as thinking very highly of 'Mr Noyes and his fine book'. Neither then nor subsequently did the English cardinal make any secret of his views: he said bluntly that he deplored alike the fact and the circumstances of the delation. On the 4th of September he saw Noyes and informed him that the document from the Holy Office had not been correctly translated. No errors of faith or morals had been detected in the book, but there might be some points of church history that would require further examination.

After that, the Holy Office prudently withdrew into its shell, leaving Cardinal Hinsley to clear up the wreckage. A special commission was set up under the Westminster board of censors. In the event they were completely satisfied with the writer's orthodoxy, and did not ask for a single alteration in the text. Some passages, however, seemed liable to misconstruction, which could be obviated if the author would write a new explanatory preface.

Noyes at once made it clear that he was perfectly satisfied with his treatment by the ecclesiastical authorities of his own country. The new preface was written, and the book was reissued some months later by a non-Catholic publishing house, Faber & Faber, to whom Sheed and Ward sold their stock for less than the cost price.

The present secretary of the Holy Office, Cardinal Ottaviani, has defended its procedures in reply to certain recent criticisms. He is reported to have said that the Holy Office judges books, not men, and that this impersonal approach, while it precludes an author from speaking in his own defence, ensures that a book shall be judged on its merits, without reference to anything that might be urged against the writer's antecedency or suspected motives. On hearing this argument, one is tempted to exclaim, with Constance:

> He talks to me that never had a son.

Has Cardinal Ottaviani ever had a book of his own denounced? It seems unlikely that any one who had would draw so artificial a distinction between a book and its author. Most writers, I think, would feel that to condemn their book is to hack at the living tissues. In any case the Holy Office does not confine its censures to books. Not many months ago it took exception to a speech made by a priest in Holland, chaplain to a university, and ordered his dismissal from the chaplaincy: an order with which the bishop of the diocese flatly refused to comply.

In addition to the censorship of books before publication, and the prohibition of condemned books afterwards, a constant unofficial pressure is kept up against the circulation of printed matter considered, often on the flimsiest grounds, to be dangerous. There are parish priests who after reading some article of which they disapprove in this or that reputable organ—it may be

the *Catholic Herald* or the *Tablet*—will take active steps
to limit its circulation in their parish. There are bishops
who will not permit the most distinguished theologians
to give lectures in their diocese. And there are religious
Orders which do not scruple to silence their members.
The Jesuit Pierre Teilhard de Chardin was thus muzzled
by his superiors, with the result that his books never saw
the light until he was dead and buried. Another Jesuit,
the poet Gerard Manley Hopkins, after reading the
manuscript of a prose work, *The Unknown Eros*, by his
fellow-poet Coventry Patmore, induced him to destroy
it, thus depriving the world of a deeply meditated and
constructive work which might indeed have been born
prematurely had it been published eighty years ago, but
would certainly have been appreciated today, for Patmore was a pioneer in that re-thinking of the theology of
sex which is now widely regarded as one of the Church's
most pressing needs.

All such interference, it need hardly be said, is intensely
repugnant to the contemporary mind. Freedom is one
of civilization's most valued gifts, and the liberty of un-
licensed printing is commonly held to be one of its surest
guarantees. The arguments for and against have been
repeated over and over again; there is no need to rehearse
them here. The Church has always tried to avoid giving
scandal to simple people, but as all men are equal in the
sight of God, even the educated should not be scandalized
too often. Moreover, human nature being what it is,
forbidden fruit will always have an attraction of its own.
The church exalts prudence as the chief of the cardinal
virtues; does not prudence suggest that the time has
come to throw these rusty weapons away?

So long as they are maintained, the church will run
the risk of being drawn from time to time into false
positions. An authority which claims to give infallible

guidance in religion and morals cannot afford to revise its judgements too frequently; yet books have been placed on the Index only to be removed in later editions. The treatise of Copernicus on the Solar System was removed in 1758. The May volume of the *Acta Sanctorum*, condemned by Clement XI at the instance of the Carmelites because it exposed the fables in which their early history had been enveloped, stayed on the Index for two hundred years until removed by a pontiff who had more respect for authentic history. To cite the most recent instance, in 1937 a book by a French Dominican Yves Congar entitled *Chrétiens Désunis* sold out almost at once, but although no theological fault could be found in it, orders from Rome forbade its reprinting. In 1950 another book of his, *Vraie et Fausse Réforme dans l'Eglise*, suffered the same fate, and for the next eight years no more appeared. But when Pope John XXIII summoned a General Council of the Church, he appointed Père Congar a consultant to the preparatory theological commission, and the illustrious Dominican is now a Master of Theology by grace of the present Pope Paul VI.

The censorship of books is also to this extent anachronistic, that the printed word is no longer the sole—perhaps no longer the most influential—vehicle for the transmission of ideas. It has been overtaken by newer modes of communication. The cinema: it might be possible in some surroundings to impose an ecclesiastical censorship of films; but what of radio and television? Dangerous ideas may find all the readier acceptance for being assimilated unconsciously or half consciously through such vivid media as these. One Protestant sect has bidden its adherents renounce them altogether, a more drastic method of shielding them from contagion than any so far contemplated by Rome; but those who obey the injunction at least do so of their own free will.

Short of such a total self-denying ordinance, the problem —if it is a problem—of insulating the faithful from ideas judged to be injurious has from sheer magnitude become insoluble.

Moreover, it could be urged that a system of censorship carried out by an administrative organization and enforced by the sanctions of canonical jurisprudence is one of those illusory short cuts which lead anywhere but to the true goal of the church's apostolate.

> There is no expeditious road
> To pack and label men for God
> And save them by the barrel load.

Faced with their immense and never-ending task of winning souls to God, churchmen throughout the centuries have yielded—and small wonder!—to the temptation of snatching at instruments really foreign to their calling. To pen the flock within high walls instead of leading them forth into green pastures; to condemn rather than to warn; to crush the heretic instead of refuting the heresy; above all, to invoke the aid of the secular power: these measures may, at certain times and seasons, be found efficacious, if only on the surface, but are they what the Church's Founder contemplated when he sent his apostles forth and bade them teach all nations?

And yet—the written word abides. It abides, and the problems it creates for Church and State cannot be dismissed as negligible, witness the efforts the State is driven to make even in free countries to control the circulation of pornography. Some people maintain that even the grossest pornography does no real harm; and they say that those who want to suppress it always do so on the ground that it corrupts other people, but not themselves. For my part, if I were cross-examined on the subject, I should have to admit that in my time I have read things which leave behind them so enduring and unpleasant an after-taste as to make me wish now that I had left them unread. Whether or not they affect one's conduct, they certainly taint the imagination, storing it with repulsive images and fantasies which obtrude themselves unbidden when one would much prefer to be intent on other things. And if the imagination can be corrupted, so too can the intellect. We smile at the founder of Positivism, Auguste Comte, for refusing to read any literature that seemed likely 'to hurt the originality and homogeneity of his meditations', but the principle of what he called 'cerebral hygiene' is not in itself absurd. Advocates of unlimited freedom argue that there is a higher moral value in resistance to harmful influences than in a purity of thought and action secured mainly by shutting them out. It may be so; but what if the noxious things refuse to be shut out? In the domains of philosophy, theology, and politics, ideas can have explosive force.

Totalitarian states recognize this, and keep a tight hold on literature which impugns their own system of ideas. The Catholic Church is not a totalitarian institution, though it has often looked like one. Essentially the Church is an association of people whose bond of union lies in certain convictions about the creation and destiny of man which they hold in common; and when confronted with ideas fundamentally incompatible with those convictions, it has an obvious right to point out the incompatibility. The real question at issue is, how should this be done?

Under the inspired leadership of Popes John XXIII and Paul VI the Church has embarked upon a far-reaching programme of reform. Dead wood is being cut away; old habits of thought are being re-examined; and

Pope Paul has made it clear that even the central administrative organs in Rome will not be immune from change. Amid this vast upheaval, which bids fair to leave a permanent impress on the religious history of mankind, the practice of censorship, if not the theory, is almost certain to be modified.

In the presence of more than two thousand bishops from all over the world the procedures of the Holy Office have been solemnly denounced by the Cardinal Archbishop of Cologne. This powerful voice from the Catholic Rhineland could be neither silenced nor ignored, and it awakened multiple echoes throughout the English-speaking world, where secret denunciations and secret trials are regarded with abhorrence as violating the principle that justice must be not only done but seen to be done. Reform in this quarter is certainly over-due, and widespread will be the disappointment if it is not effected in the near future. A change of direction is perhaps already foreshadowed in the action taken recently over posthumous works of Teilhard de Chardin. This Jesuit priest was a distinguished palaeontologist, not a theologian. His attempts to bridge the gap between religion and natural science were novel enough to excite alarm in certain quarters, and not so long ago the alarmists might well have secured a condemnation from Rome; but this time the Holy Office has contented itself with issuing a warning measured enough to prevent Teilhard's readers from swallowing his theories whole, and leaving open the possibility of further discussion.

The relatively innocuous diocesan censorship of books as yet unpublished may survive under mitigated rules, but the Index of Prohibited Books will surely be allowed to die a natural death. Its pages are littered with forgotten controversies: who cares nowadays about the

Synod of Pistoia? In the realm of imaginative writing
securus judicat orbis terrarum; if a book is a recognized
classic of European literature, what practical end is
served by putting it under a ban? Between the magnitude of the penalty decreed for those of the faithful who
read it, and the occasional naughtiness that can be found
in such a romance as *The Three Musketeers*, the dis-
proportion is so enormous as to be patently absurd; it is
like using a sledgehammer where a nutcracker would
more than suffice. An authority which magnifies
peccadillos into mortal sins puts an unwarrantable
strain on tender consciences, and in the long run
undermines respect for its own decrees. As for the more
austere branches of literature, how many of the faithful
are tempted to take the *Critique of Pure Reason* for their
bedside reading? The student of philosophy can hardly
afford to neglect it, but when he learns that the Holy See
has judged Kant's philosophy erroneous, he will also
require to be told just where the errors lie.

For in the long run bad ideas can only be overcome by
good ideas, and to condemn the bad is to discharge only
one half of the teacher's responsibility. It is not enough
to put the *Critique of Pure Reason* on the Index and leave
the faithful reciting the Apostles Creed: the antidote is
too indirect. Those who can read the book at all could
also read intelligent criticisms of it if they were told where
to find them. To blot out one side of the debate was not
the way of the Catholic Church in the great days of the
Schoolmen. In their pages thesis and antithesis both
found a place. 'It seems that there is no God', writes St
Thomas Aquinas, 'for the following reasons . . .' And
after stating the grounds of atheism quite dispassionately,
he proceeds to counter them with positive arguments
pointing the other way.

In past centuries the Popes have been enlightened

patrons of art and scholarship. John Lingard, the priest who wrote the first *History of England* objectively based on research into primary sources, was honoured by Rome with three doctorates, and only the untimely death of Leo XIII prevented him from receiving a cardinal's hat. In this century the one English historian to be similarly honoured was Gasquet, a far less happy choice. From time to time some good creature who has given years of devoted service in the sacristy receives— and who will grudge it?—a cross or a medal from Rome; but it is possible for a Catholic to edit the liveliest of Catholic journals for twenty years and more, or to produce an historical masterpiece, or to write novels and plays which enjoy a worldwide circulation, without receiving any mark of papal esteem. The reason for this neglect is not that the Popes are unwilling to bestow honour where honour is due, but that they depend for information on local advisers who, immersed as they are in the problems of day-to-day administration, have no leisure to weigh up intellectual merit; some of them, indeed, might not recognize it if it stared them in the face. Yet a Holy See acting once more as a fountain of honour to encourage sound learning and original creative work could do much more for the human spirit than a Holy See raising a purely negative voice from time to time in condemnation of an immoral or heretical book.

At this time above all, when reform is in the air, and the whole system inherited from the Council of Trent under review, there is need of the fullest and frankest discussion. Immense issues are at stake. The Church has undertaken to enter into a dialogue with the contemporary world in terms which the contemporary mind can understand; but dialogue cannot prosper in a climate of repression. Repression, in any case, is born of fear, and fear is proverbially a bad counsellor. Pope John was not afraid. In that brief reign of his, the most glorious in modern history, one thing stands out above all: his total assurance that in confronting the modern world the Church needs no other armoury than that of her abiding truth.

Freedom
and the Individual

ROSEMARY HAUGHTON

IF the Catholic Church were brought to trial on a charge of restricting the freedom of the human spirit, the counsel for the prosecution would be likely to come into court in a rather more cheerful frame of mind than his opponent. But it is unlikely that a trial would be thought necessary if we in the West were not so addicted to the forms of justice that even a prisoner who has committed a crime publicly, repeatedly, and with a running commentary of self-justification must still stand trial before sentence may be passed. Other civilizations might consider that summary execution or, more humanely, strict confinement in a mental hospital, would be more appropriate.

The belief that the Catholic Church is the enemy of freedom has become the first article of the anti-Catholic creed. At a time when free discussion and liberty of conscience were not greatly encouraged by other Christian bodies either, the immorality of the Scarlet Woman was the number one accusation. Times change, and a charge of depravity would not cut much ice nowadays. But it has been found that the statement that 'Catholics are not allowed to think for themselves' makes an excellent substitute. No need is felt to prove such a statement. Everyone knows it is true, and 'everyone' includes a good many contented Catholics.

People who have Catholic friends are aware that some of these discuss their Church and her teaching in a manner sometimes critical, and refuse to be flattened by the clerical steam-roller. Does this prove that Catholics may, after all, exercise their God-given intellects and assume personal responsibility? Not at all. It only proves that these particular Catholics are not toeing the party line. They get away with it because the Church, at present lacking temporal power, cannot prosecute them. If they are seen to practise their religion regularly and with apparent sincerity, this only means that they are too much afraid of hell, the Holy Office, or the parish priest to abandon their religion altogether. It is a recognized fact that really faithful Catholics are those who are too stupid or too docile to think about or question anything the Church tells them! They just believe, and do as they are told. This may be a feeble and slightly sub-human way to live, but this, it is said (by quite intelligent people), is what the Catholic Church demands of her children and it is by exacting this, by means of a mixture of threats and sweets, that she has managed to keep her hold over so many people for so long.

This picture of how the Catholic Church appears to millions outside the fold is not, alas, an exaggeration. Some well-disposed intellectuals, impressed by the spiritual stature of certain Catholic saints and sages, have struggled manfully with the contradiction between such clear evidence of human magnificence and the known fact that Catholicism confines and enslaves the human spirit. To explain this one or two theories have been developed. One states that intellectual imprisonment may be considered worthwhile by some people because it does away with the need to search for truth, and so frees the soul to soar upwards—presumably because it has nowhere else to go. There is an element of truth in this, for a total committal is the prerequisite of all real love, human and divine, and intellectual uncertainty inhibits this. But anyway it is a very satisfactory theory because it leaves the non-mystic non-Catholic with the comfortable feeling that he himself has sacrificed a great reward for the sake of preserving his intellectual freedom.

Another explanation is that the great Catholic mystics obeyed and believed the Church out of a mixture of fear and ignorance (the latter being excusable in the ages of unenlightenment), but surreptitiously, and in all good faith, slipped beyond her grasp into the higher spiritual regions. The assumption here is that they were only Catholics because everyone was, and would have been greater and better mystics if they had not been. This theory is in some respects even more comforting, because one can admire the Catholic mystics, and yet feel that if one were so inclined one could be wiser, saintlier, and even more mystical than they, lacking their doctrinal handicap.

Now the really awful thing about all this is not the fact that people think like this. It is that the Catholic Church should present to the world—the world Christ died for—an image of herself which allows or even obliges honest and intelligent people to adopt such grotesque mental and spiritual attitudes. But perhaps still worse than the effect of this image on those outside the Roman Communion is the fact that vast numbers of Catholics are not only content to accept as true an image substantially similar though more attractively dressed, but even exult in it. Reactions to recent arguments about whether the wave of ecumenical activity has reduced the number of conversions to the Catholic faith have confirmed what was already clear enough, that not a few converts have come into the Church because they wanted to be told what to believe and so be relieved of the heavy responsibility of personal search and commitment.

To many Catholics, both converts and 'cradle' Catholics, the new tendency to examine old teachings, to reassert the primacy of conscience (even erroneous conscience), to seek for contact with non-Catholics and to give their attitudes and teaching a favourable hearing is frankly terrifying. They feel the Rock shuddering under them, their safe refuge seems about to erupt. These are not necessarily cowardly or feeble people. To many people whose grasp of their faith may be deeper than their religious education has given them words to express, the unease caused by the apparent reversal of old principles is not a matter for shame. It simply indicates that they have not been educated to be anything but passive in religious matters. But there are others for whom the total lack of change in the Church, which they exalt into a virtue, is a refuge from themselves and from God. The freedom implied in the 'new' ideas threatens to destroy their image of themselves and expose them to self-knowledge. It is all too easy for them to justify this feeling by reference to the image of Catholicism described above.

This fear that many Catholics have of 'too much'

freedom is rooted in the same error that makes non-Catholics accuse the Church of attempting to destroy the essential human dignity of personal freedom and responsibility. It consists in seeing the whole matter as a struggle between two forces that are of their nature opposed: the forces of freedom and authority. Since these can never be reconciled they must discover some method of coexistence. Supporters of either side agree that authority should not be absolute or freedom unlimited if a society is to survive, so the struggle is over the amount of space that freedom may claim or authority allow. The deep Catholic awareness of the need for authority in the proper sense can, and does, lead Catholics to assume that an almost limitless political-type authority is proper to those who are called to govern the Church. Those outside the Church, convinced of the fundamental value of human liberty, see this authority in the same terms (no others are offered them), and naturally deplore it.

It is this either/or presentation of the problem of personal freedom in the Church of Rome that makes the image of a trial almost inevitable. The whole discussion could be conducted on those lines, presenting the case for and against the Church as a holy tyrant, and such a course is not without usefulness if only because it demonstrates the limitations of this point of view.

Called as a witness for the prosecution we would probably find St Ignatius of Antioch, who could easily be made to appear as a fanatical supporter of the idea of total submission to the bishop. 'When you submit to the bishop as to Jesus Christ, I see you no longer living like men but like Jesus Christ who died for us.' The way in which he and St Cyprian and others of the same vintage exalted obedience to authority in the Church can be used by Catholics and non-Catholics alike as evidence of the sheep-like qualities required of good Catholics. Any attempt by the defence to show that what these Saints required from those who obey was something as different from passive docility as the controlled and flexible response of a trained dancer is from the uncomprehending reactions of a performing seal would probably only confuse a twentieth century jury, whose members can only understand what they have been taught to think of as the 'plain facts'—that is, objective, exterior actions.

A more hopeful witness from the defence point of view would be St Augustine, with his insistence that he, though a bishop, is 'a sinner with you', 'a disciple and a hearer of the Gospel together with you'. It would be possible for the prosecution to try to show that this humility was accidental, and due to Augustine's sense of his earlier moral shortcomings, but the fact remains that he confided in the laity his hopes and fears and plans and the reasons for them in a way that is unheard of nowadays and which certainly seems to have been an invitation to them to co-operate freely and not as slaves.

Witnesses from the Middle Ages would certainly be to the advantage of the prosecution. The virtual exclusion of laymen from influence in the Church (however historically understandable), the welding of Church and State into a sovereign system with absolute rights and the development of Canon Law as the natural result of this—these things created a pattern which has been widely accepted as the 'normal' Catholic system, from which other ways of organizing and considering people in relation to the mission of the Church have been seen as temporary and unfortunate deviations. In such an atmosphere, 'freedom' must inevitably appear as disloyalty. This tendency was canonized in St Thomas à Becket, whose single-minded zeal for the unfettered power of the Church might make one feel that the verdict was settled before the trial was half over.

Saint Thomas Aquinas could easily be a key witness for the prosecution, lending his enormous prestige to the contemporary attitude towards those who did not stick to the party line. 'When the heretic's guilt is so well known, and people find it so loathsome, that he has no-one to defend him—or at any rate not such as would lead to schism—there must be no leniency in his punishment.'

Although this might be damaging to his case, the counsel for the defence need not be too cast down because he could cancel out the force of this statement by showing that it is incompatible with certain basic principles which the witness has stated and supported on other occasions. 'If a man acts against his conscience he sins', even when what his conscience orders him to do is objectively wrong. So that, according to the statement quoted, 'there must be no leniency' in punishing a man who refuses to sin by disobeying his (objectively erroneous) conscience.

The prosecution would be much happier with succeeding centuries, especially after the Reformation, when the rights of conscience, until then repeatedly affirmed by the Church in theory if not consistently respected by Catholics in practice, were allowed to drop out of sight. The emphasis on discipline, obedience, and submission as conditions of unity and strength became almost an obsession in the Catholic Church, in reaction to the Reformers' claim for the absolute freedom of the Christian from any religious authority but the inner compulsion of conscience formed by the word of God in Scripture.

There is plenty of evidence for the increasing centralization of the Church: the gradual loss of prestige by bishops who became in the end little more than local mouth-pieces of the Pope, the suppression of all original thought, the craze for uniformity, the rigid legalism, the intellectual obscurantism coupled with a sprouting of curious devotions, and the tightening grip of a censorship that became less and less rational, more and more fear-ridden and close. These tendencies, reaching their furthest development in the nineteenth and early twentieth centuries, were 'crystallized' by the growth of the power and prestige of the Roman Curia using its pseudo-papal authority to give to all these things the status of permanent components of Catholic life and thought.

All this looks bad for the defence. It could certainly demonstrate that the hair-raising items of Pius IXth's notorious 'Syllabus of Errors' do not sound nearly so violent when they are restored to the context from which they were plucked for convenience of tabulation. But nothing can undo the damaging effect of their first pronouncement, the solemn assertion that Catholics must repudiate as subversive such opinions as:

> Every man is free to embrace and profess the religion he considers to be the true one by the light of reason.
>
> Protestantism is simply a different form of the one true Christian religion, and in it it is possible to be as pleasing to God as in the Catholic Church.
>
> In our age there is no longer any point in regarding the Catholic religion as the one State religion to the exclusion of all other forms of worship.
>
> Therefore it has been quite right to provide by law in certain Catholic countries that foreigners taking up residence there should be allowed freedom to exercise their own particular form of public worship.
>
> The Roman Pontiff can and should reconcile him-

self to and compromise with progress, liberalism and modern civilisation.

This shattering pronouncement still has the power to send cold shivers down the spines of Catholics, and it would seem hardly possible to make out a case for the existence of freedom in a body whose head has described as 'a false and absurd maxim, or rather madness, [the idea that] every individual should be given and guaranteed freedom of conscience, that most contagious of errors.'

Yet the case for the defence is not lost, for even in this period voices can be heard that proclaim (very softly at first) a different message, and soon there come crowding into the witness box a succession of distinguished scholars, theologians and even popes, asserting with increasing resonance the reversal of opinions once considered essential to Catholicism. One witness after another can be heard enthusiastically welcoming the separation of Church and State, freedom of religion, the advances of science, democracy, biblical criticism, a responsible laity, local adaptations of the liturgy, friendly contact with heretics (now renamed 'separated brethren').

So it seems that the Catholic Church has a new look, and has suffered a change of heart. Or has she? The defence says yes, and her admitted failures in the past were due to bad influences, difficult social conditions, etc. The prosecution says no, her past misdeeds show her real nature, and all the present talk of freedom and responsibility is mere opportunism. She will swim with the tide of opinion, biding her time, until she is in a position to assert her power once more. If that ever happens we shall get rack and thumbscrews, say her enemies; a nice safe refuge from the wicked world, say some of her children.

But when all the witnesses and the counsel have been heard, and the case summed up as fairly as possible, the verdict will probably be pronounced one way or the other in accordance with the prejudices the jury started off with before they came into court. Little can be decided in this way because, interesting as the centuries-old tension may be historically and psychologically, its presentation in terms of for and against is misleading. It is misleading because we are made to see the Church as a political entity, in which context alone such a struggle makes sense. It is the fault of Catholics—in this matter the fundamental fault—that we have allowed this view of freedom versus authority in the Church to be accepted almost to the exclusion of any other, not only by those outside the Roman Communion but almost universally by Catholics themselves.

We cannot decide whether or not the Catholic Church is the home or the enemy of freedom by weighing up her historical record but only by trying to see whether true personal freedom is of the essence of Catholicism as properly understood, or whether it is something that has been dragged into the structure of Catholic life by those who, as human beings, value it and want to reconcile it with a religion which has no real place for it.

What the poor historical record of the Church in this matter can do is to show that defective ideas about freedom led to the suppression of freedom, in practice if not in theory.

But there are two kinds of freedom in question here which must not be confused—exterior and interior. The degree of exterior freedom can be determined by reading history. This kind of freedom allows people to express outwardly the ideas and ideals they cherish. This is what most people mean by freedom, and it is essential because the restriction of it by the use of fear (induced fantasy fears or actual threats) restricts also the use of interior freedom. But it is interior freedom which is most important, the freedom of the individual's mind and soul to discover itself. It also means the freedom to respond to the love of God, for there can be no love without freedom. This is not as simple as it sounds, because in practice the personal use of freedom is restricted by circumstances (interior and exterior) to an extent which makes many people doubt if there can be such a thing as a free act. It is circumscribed, in fact, by the human condition of ignorance of self and of others, by the fears that grow from this ignorance, and the intellectual and emotional distortions that attempt to balance the fears. So that in a real sense no one is wholly free this side of the grave. This does not mean that we cannot exercise freedom at all, but simply that its effective exercise depends on the degree of self-knowledge, of spiritual maturity, reached by the individual. But even in the immature there is the pushing towards effective freedom, and this in itself and even in its lack of success, is part of the process of self-learning which increases the area of effective personal freedom. But if freedom implies self-knowledge it means something which is almost the opposite of what most people think of as freedom: the freedom to do wrong. Because the more you know of yourself, the more you understand what kind of thing you are, the *less* likely you are to mistake the purpose of your existence and make the wrong choices. Making the wrong choice is not a sign of interior freedom, but of lack of the self-knowledge which alone makes freedom possible. On the other hand making the wrong choices is often a means of discovering that they *are* wrong and therefore of growing in self-knowledge, and this is where exterior freedom comes in, the freedom to make mistakes and discover for yourself that they are mistakes. But growth by trial and error could be terribly risky and lengthy, hence the need for authority to act as a guide in the pursuit of self-knowledge: to say, this is what you are, this is what you are for. This is the kind of authority that fosters interior freedom, this is the real function of exterior authority in the Church. The freedom the Christian must insist on is the freedom of the spirit, freedom to respond to God's love by complete self-giving. Anything whatever that prevents this is wrong, whether it be the fear of physical pain or the fear of losing a reassuring image of oneself or even (in one peculiar sense) the fear of God. Authority in the Church should be there to support and guide the use of interior freedom, and this is how the holiest and most thoughtful of her children have always understood it. Why, then, has authority been so often abused and interior freedom cramped by the restriction of its exterior manifestation?

The understanding of the interrelation of exterior and interior freedom is only partly an intellectual matter. It can be realized without being fully or explicitly expressed. But if the expression is deficient at any one period of the Church's history, many people will get no further than this deficient expression will take them; so that, corporately, the Church may accept a 'wrong' idea which is not compatible with her true self. The understanding of the relations between interior and exterior freedom has been of slow growth in the Church, as can be seen by the self-contradictory nature of St Thomas's various pronouncements on freedom of conscience. A partly 'political' attitude to authority in the Church was inevitable in the context of the ideal of 'Christendom'. But although this ideal has had to be abandoned (reluctantly) the suspicion of exterior freedom remains.

We say: the Church is given authority by God to

proclaim and interpret his revelation and his law; her subjects listen, believe and obey, and by their obedience show their love of God. It sounds all right, if a bit dull. After all, Christ said, 'If you love me, keep my commandments.' But note the priority. The usual Catholic interpretation of this (in practice and often enough in so many words) is 'keep the commandments, especially those of outward observance, and we'll reckon that as love of God.' Subtly, and with the best intentions, the priorities have been reversed. And it is precisely at this point, in this almost unnoticed and even in a sense justifiable reversal of values, that the barren struggle between a political-type freedom and authority begins.

In trying to get away from the political or juridical understanding of freedom in the Church it seems helpful to look at the matter as one of 'personal' response both *by* the Church to Christ her head, and *in* the Church by the Christian who needs to find and obey Christ in her. The two complementary concepts of the Church need to be used like stereoscopic lenses to give a three dimensional picture: that of the Church as Christ's body, an organism living by his life and called to do his work, and that of the Church as the Bride, that is as an image of the redeemed, other than but closely united with Christ and responding to his redeeming grace.

The historical attitudes of Catholics towards personal freedom seem to follow in an interesting way the typical pattern of personal development, and while it can be misleading to push any analogy too far the parallel between individual spiritual growth and that of the Church is illuminating, for it seems to show *why* authority has been abused, exterior freedom curtailed and interior freedom inhibited in the Church, often with the best intentions.

The Church is people, and each one bears in himself the pattern of interrelated functions which we transfer to our understanding of the 'person' which is the Church. It is at the level of the psychology of the individual Christian that the whole question of authority and freedom must find its solution, or fail to find one and fall back on the choice between exterior submission or opposition.

The early Church was not troubled by the problem of freedom because the fresh joy of her redemption lifted her, for the time being, beyond the influences of her heredity and of the culture in which she was destined to develop. Freedom was not a problem but a fact, effective in a joyful response to the gift of God's love and forgiveness. Authority was an opportunity for service, by guiding and enlightening, and the response to that service was a deep respect and love on the part of those who obeyed, and so grew in self-knowledge and freedom.

This freshness and spontaneity, the sense of freedom and the true though unreflecting realization that this freedom is to be used for loving—this is characteristic of the youthful enthusiasm of what is sometimes called 'first conversion', but is better compared to the effect of first falling in love. For the time being the factors that normally restrict interior freedom seem to be ineffective. It is this sense of liberation which gives people in this state the feeling that they are, as never before, wholly themselves. They admit no restrictions, they feel capable of anything. The 'Acts' breathes this confidence, and it is continually breaking out in St Paul's letters.

At this stage interior freedom is deeply felt but not intellectually understood. The very perfection of the interrelation of freedom and authority, in the individual and in the 'person' of the Church, makes such an under-

standing almost impossible. Therefore it is psychologically absurd to expect at this stage of the Church's
history an explicit manifesto in support of exterior
freedom (the freedom to make mistakes in good faith,
without being regarded as a traitor). But the seeds of
misunderstanding are there, for the spontaneous and
loving response to the demands of God's love as presented
by the teaching Church make questioning or criticism
seem monstrous, in the same way that to people newly
in love any doubt of the perfection of the beloved seems
treacherous, something to be fought off as long as
possible.

In the next stage of the Church's development, when
growth in size and the need to cope with the practical
details of being a Christian in everyday political life
made it more and more difficult to maintain the original
spontaneous harmony; authority in the Church became
gradually divided between the mainly administrative
authority of the bishop and the spiritual, charismatic
authority represented by the monastic ideal. There was
great overlapping, and this simplification is in any case
crude, but it will serve. The response of the faithful (now
including hordes of still semi-pagan barbarians) to the
latter retained, astonishingly, some of the wholeness and
spontaneous freedom of earlier centuries, it was a
response of the heart. But obedience to ecclesiastical
orders began to assume more and more the character of
merely external obedience, unrelated to 'the spirit of
sonship'.[1] The emphasis shifted with time to this type
of passive obedience, for the influences of heredity were
reasserting themselves. The legacy of Judaism, which
emphasised an obedience that 'held us captive',[2] shaped
an attitude that demanded unreflecting submission to

[1] Rom. 8. 15.
[2] Rom. 7. 6.

an authority that began to think of itself not as acting simply as an instrument of divine authority, with all that that implies of the need for humility and purity of life, but rather as exercising a fully possessed mandate from God. The influence of the centralized, authoritarian, Imperial system of government was not without importance in developing this tendency; it was later reinforced by the need to keep the masses of wild half-Christians in some sort of order.

This stage also is paralleled in individual development, when the resplendent goal turns out to be less easily attainable than had at first appeared. Practical difficulties of adjustment are becoming apparent, and the temptation is to give in, to lose sight of the first vision of freedom and love and compromise with 'reality'. If this is resisted then what usually happens is that the strength of the whole person is concentrated on attaining its goal by the use of all the resources of its own will-power, directed by its own intelligence. This intelligence is as yet unsubtle and given to drastic over-simplifications, so that even the final goal of all this striving, first glimpsed in its intuitive simplicity, is rationalized to conform with the forces of heredity and of the need to compensate for accidental difficulties and deprivations imposed by environment. Enthusiastic adolescents (spiritual adolescents can be any age) try to coerce themselves, to break through by sheer will-power to the goal on which they have set their hearts, and it is tempting to see this tendency in the Church of the Middle Ages, with its vision of 'Christendom' as a step towards the Kingdom of Heaven on earth, and its typically adolescent intolerance of criticism, or of contrary opinions. The other's limited freedom *cannot* be recognized because the restrictions of one's own freedom are not recognized, and every act is held to be fully responsible. Hence, in the 'person' of the Church, savage intolerance of heresy and a staggeringly *simpliste* attitude to problems of conscience.

But the goal thus conceived turns out to be a mirage, for these fierce acts of will are not truly free. They are dictated by preconceptions whose nature is determined by emotional needs. Their strength is the strength of those needs, and their goal is an image designed to satisfy them. This disillusion may lead to a collapse of the overdriven will. Or it can lead to the virtual repudiation of the original vision, so that only dogged loyalty supports the necessity of daily living. Or there may begin a period of apparently fruitless striving to regain the lost vision, and often these latter two exist and alternate in the same person. In any case the part played by adherence to external rules is important. These may be seen as a sufficient substitute for a love which is no longer a perceptible motive power, or they may be obscurely desired as the framework upon which a personal response may be shaped until it can do without this support though it retains its shape. When an external code is regarded as an absolute good, even when divorced from personal understanding and acceptance, the personality is fixed at a stage of immaturity, and generally makes a virtue of it. When such a code is understood (however dimly) as a means of personal response, then every act of adherence or even attempted adherence to it is an exercise of the feeble but surviving capacity for free action, even when the particular attempt fails.

These strands of behaviour can be discerned in the history of the Catholic Church after the upheaval of the Reformation. The failure to reach by sheer human effort the illusory goal of which 'Christendom' was the image led to the Reformers' emphasis on justification, when the overworked 'will' had collapsed. There were those, too, who gave up the struggle to solve the problem of freedom as Christians, and humanism was born with its more limited and therefore attainable goals.

Within the Catholic Church the emphasis on rigid discipline, defence against attack, and reliance on external rules was not the only reaction. A more mature, though slightly desperate, courage is also apparent, a determination to make the God-given 'system' work, even though its purpose and nature seem less clear cut than formerly, and many new doubts blur the outlines of the design. As in the individual, this new 'dark age' of the Church seems to have been the necessary prelude to a great break-through. During the post-Reformation centuries there is ample evidence of an unease among many holy and sensitive people (Newman is only one example), a real but still obscure search for the right use of a freedom which was certainly present but largely ineffective since all evidence of a desire for it was regarded as dangerous sabotage and promptly suppressed. The nineteenth century witnessed a dramatic heightening of the tension between the strong urge towards a total response to an ancient but newly realized vocation, whatever the risks involved, and the frightened clinging to a traditional, rigid and as far as possible unexamined pattern of belief and behaviour. The longing to break free seemed doomed, for the very existence of the Church appeared to depend on the preservation of this pattern. Hence the violent and indiscriminate condemnation of the Modernist movement. The same mounting conflict can be observed in the process of personal maturation, the long process of discovering the mode of action which is proper to a human being and without which he is not really free at all.

Saint Augustine's is perhaps the most famous 'conversion story'. He recorded in detail the various stages leading, through many years, to the moment of actual conversion, especially the long period of unsuccessful attempts to 'break through' to freedom. But countless other diaries and biographies record a similar pattern, which is not exclusively a Christian one. The word 'conversion' has become so cluttered with religious and frequently distasteful associations that its real meaning has become obscured. It might be described as the moment at which the struggle towards self-knowledge reaches the point of breakthrough. It always happens in response to some kind of external challenge, which may appear quite accidental and have no religious signific-ance. But the moment of freedom is perceptible, and not only that, but the degree of freedom and the remain-ing area of unfreedom become perceptible too, whereas before it was possible to be ignorant of the absence of a freedom which remained merely an abstraction to be argued about. Equally familiar and real in such records is the sense that this act which liberates is not merely a reaction to the accidental challenge of circumstances but is also a response to a demand external to the self, whatever name you choose to give to its source. This freeing and free act is felt as part of a dialogue, for which the ancient and fitting image is that of sexual love. But although the act of will which effects the breakthrough to freedom is made in response to what appears to be an exterior command, the person is able to respond because that which he experiences as exterior is related to something in himself which has the power to order the obedience of the whole self. This interior 'authority' can only act properly in response to the 'command' from outside. The attempt to use this 'authority' other-wise than in response to the other side of the 'dialogue' ends in that parody of real freedom which is typified by the 'hero' figure of antiquity, responsible to none, ruthless in his dedication to a self-chosen purpose, and doomed to ultimate futility by forces that are after all stronger than he.

This is the perennial temptation of institutional authority, from which the Catholic Church has not been exempt, as history shows.

It seems hardly necessary to examine in detail the parallel between the typical process of individual 'conversion' and what has happened to the Catholic Church in the last few years. Like all conversions, this one was preceded by a long period of apparent immobility. Yet all the time the forces below the surface, the Church's 'subconscious', were altering her from within. The external accidental stimulus has been the increasing challenge to her very existence offered by the progress of science, technology and non-Christian ideologies. All the great movements of human progress had begun and continued not only outside the area of the Church's influence but usually in the teeth of her frantic opposition. The dignity of human liberty had been proclaimed by men and women who owed no allegiance to the Church and who saw in her the enemy of all that they cherished. Meanwhile the Church had made hysterical scenes and alternately stormed at and appealed to the consciences that her every act served to alienate further. Finally she was forced to see herself as she appeared to others: possessive, self-centred, intolerant, fearful, decked in the trappings of a power and beauty that had vanished. The shock of that vision brought her to her moment of truth.

Those (whether they approve or not) who attribute the current revolution in the Catholic Church to the pressures of external events and see in it an abandonment of ancient principles are to this extent quite right. The crisis was precipitated by an exterior challenge as it must be. But the 'conversion' only follows when the exterior threat forces a recognition of the necessity of making a choice: whether to draw back, repudiate, consolidate and stagnate, or whether to take the plunge into the unknown, risk everything, and trust.

The only really free act is an act of love. It is expressed in this complete trust, it is a 'going out', and after this the defences are down, freedom is an effective and perceptible fact, not a movement which remains at least partially frustrated by ignorance and fear.

But this freedom is not simply the recovery of the unreflecting spontaneity of first love. It is much more, for it is the freedom of self-understanding, stripped of illusions, moulded by suffering, enlightened by experience, even the experience of failure and of misdirected energies. It is the freedom of maturity.

In the individual this is only the beginning of a new phase, for the new self-knowledge must be extended, the strength acquired through suffering tested on new work, the freedom exercised. Above all the 'dialogue' must continue to direct the use of the interior 'authority'.

In the Church the newly rediscovered dialogue between the authority of God and the corresponding authority within the 'person' of the Church should be the touchstone that tests the authenticity of her response to her vocation. Can authority become once more one of service to individual self-knowledge and therefore knowledge of God, undertaken in dialogue with its source and pattern, Christ? Can freedom become the response of loving obedience, on the pattern of Christ's example, who was freely and totally obedient, 'even to death'? This is the only kind of authority which is compatible with the freedom of the sons of God, and this is the only kind of freedom whose fullest expression is obedience. This obedience to inner truth must be not only felt but understood in its dual reality as response to the exemplar, Christ, and as the moulding to its proper shape of the human psyche in relation to God in whose image it is formed.

Anything that really helps self-knowledge and strips away illusion can bring effective freedom closer. The depths opened up by modern psychology ought to assist the intelligent Catholic to understand better the stages of his own growth towards maturity, and to see how true authority in the Church can help this development of interior freedom both positively by setting out its nature and purpose and negatively by guaranteeing that exterior freedom from unnecessary fear that makes interior freedom easier.

It is because of the 'conversion' of the Church that a conscious understanding of the relation of exterior to interior freedom is now possible. The new self-knowledge so painfully acquired should help the Church as a whole to appreciate the moral futility of obedience that is anything except a free response. It has been, is, and always will be the Church's task to announce clearly the revelation of God about himself and about the true and proper shape of human nature, but perhaps only now is it possible to realise how greatly fear inhibits the human ability to respond with the freedom of love to the demands made by the Church in the name of her founder.

The Church does not consist of fully mature human beings. At any one time only a minority will have anything like a full understanding of the free nature of the truly Christian response to authority. 'Love God and do as you will,' said St Augustine, but learning to love God is a slow business; we mostly love a glorified version of ourselves and call it God. In the process of unfrocking this idol and uncovering in ourselves the truer image which is the pattern of our being, adherence to the framework of a system of belief and behaviour which exteriorly expresses the real nature of the unperceived interior pattern is essential. But such an adherence must be encouraged as the exercise of an as yet imperfect freedom. Then it is part of the way to spiritual maturity, not a substitute for it.

Even if it seems that the Catholic Church really has been 'changed', as the revivalists say, we cannot assume that progress hereafter will be automatic. There could be a relapse, a loss of vision, even now, and the guilt of that failure would be very great. Failure to explore courageously the implications and scope of the freedom so hardly won could lead to a new and worse decay.

It is tempting for Catholics who have longed for this day to rejoice in the new freedom and underestimate the magnitude of the work still to be done and the precariousness of the victory so far won. It is not for nothing that many outside the Church refuse to wax enthusiastic over the apparent change of heart. The old psychological habits are still there, ready to take over again, given the chance, and all of them are connected with the misunderstanding and therefore the restriction of Christian freedom. If, as I have suggested, the bad record of Catholics in the past was due to an imperfect understanding of the relation between interior and exterior freedom, leading to too great an emphasis on purely exterior obedience, then the great need is to examine the life of the Church today and see whether and where freedom is still misunderstood and obedience still equated with passivity, and then what can be done about it. If the following (extremely curtailed) catalogue of horrors makes Catholics bristle defensively then they are showing a different spirit from that of many great figures in the opening sessions of the Council.

For those who really love the Church are not afraid to confess her guilt, which is ours too, and declare a firm purpose of amendment.

Sins against freedom abound, and sins against interior freedom have grown out of the denial of exterior freedom in the past. Exterior freedom—of a kind—we now have, but the restrictions on interior freedom are brought about by other and subtler methods. Physical force is 'out' (except apparently in Sicily and Malta) but emotional and moral blackmail is very much 'in'.

Also still in fashion is the habit of mind by which those in authority in the Church do not deliberately deny freedom to the laity but simply assume that it does not and cannot exist. And the laity, in large numbers, make the same assumption. Instances of responsible and intelligent co-operation between clergy and laity are loudly welcomed, but their very newsworthiness makes one suspicious. It is depressing but true that the vast majority of Catholics are totally unaware of the significance of the work of Vatican II, and some are only dimly aware that a Council, whatever that may be, is going on. Intelligent response is simply not expected, mute obedience is all that is required. In the last few years I have heard with my own ears two remarks from the pulpit which are not at all unusual. This one: 'When the priest speaks to you he is in the place of God. Whatever he says you must believe and obey, for it is God who speaks through him.' (This priest was a charming and holy man who took his responsibility as *vox Dei* with commendable seriousness.) And when the Decree on the Liturgy was published the fact was announced from a pulpit (well, that's something: it was often ignored) with the comment '. . . but all that concerns you now is . . .' followed by a tiny alteration in the rubrics which was to be immediately effective. The sheep in the pews need know nothing until the time comes for them to be herded somewhere or other, without explanation or preparation. Then they will no doubt go there, in a properly sheep-like spirit. Thus is the work of the Council nullified.

'If we obey under constraint, by routine, without the child's spontaneity of love, then we are servile men, Old Testament men, for whom Christ has not yet died and risen.'[1] Habit is useful, even essential, in order to bring us to the point of doing something with the minimum of wasted effort. But an action done solely out of habit can have no moral or formative value, it can never be an act of love. A good routine can be the foundation on which Christian life can be built, but a foundation without a house on it is not a dwelling for the free Spirit of God by which we cry 'Father!' It is only a platform for trivialities and silly passions to picnic on. Yet in the upbringing of Catholic children (and Catholics are too often treated as children all their lives) it is habit and routine which are insisted on, and it is to the need to form habits early and bring them up in a 'Christian routine' that appeal is made in order to justify the overwhelming emphasis on Catholic schools. The habit of going to Mass 'and the sacraments' (note that 'and'), the habit of family prayers, the habit of saying the rosary—all that matters is just doing these things, they become magic spells that will get us to heaven without any real personal commitment at all, or so one would think. Continued adherence to exterior observances can indeed be true evidence of a love that for the time has lost all spontaneity and seems pointless and even repugnant but will not give up. But observances that are *merely* habitual are morally null.

The coercion of consciences is not exceptional. The Monday morning questioning of school-children about

[1] Dunwell: 'In the Redeeming Christ', *Christian Obedience.*

Sunday Mass attendance goes on: the cunning learn to lie and the brave to associate defiance of the Church with freedom and self-respect. As they grow up, the children learn to see passive submission as the hall-mark of the good Catholic. There can be no love without freedom, and submission can only be Christian when it is loving and therefore free. But those parents who would prefer to take their children away from such influences are branded as traitors.

By the time they are grown up, Catholics thus educated are virtually incapable of a free response to God's love in the strictly religious sphere, though God can and does elicit in a thousand other ways the loving response which cannot be made in the context of a religion which is all 'duty'. So the faithful must be made to adhere to the Church's teaching and commands by other methods. Threats of hell are far from uncommon and Purgatory is presented by kindly teachers and preachers in terms that make it appear that there isn't much to choose between the two.

More subtly, Catholics are made to feel guilty about the sufferings of Christ, so that 'moral' behaviour becomes an attempt to quiet a guilty conscience (often a false one at that). The Passion of Christ, which should evoke an outgoing compassion of free and self-forgetting love, is used to imprison consciences in a squirrel-cage of selfish guilt.

Exaggeration of personal responsibility grew from a failure (understandable when psychology as we use the term was unknown) to recognize the straitened conditions in which free will has to operate in fallen human beings. Among Catholic teachers and writers, clerical and lay, this leads to the assumption that everyone (Catholic or not) who acts in a manner contrary to the norms of Christian morality is in a state of sin. This attitude is justified by the flat statement: 'They have free will'. Any attempt to understand the motives and states of mind that can lead to objectively immoral acts and reduce or even wipe out personal guilt is regarded as a deliberate attempt to undermine Christian and moral standards.

The same doctrine of total responsibility justifies the sort of moral blackmail which is still not unheard of at Catholic missions. The missioner's aim seems to be to persuade his hearers of their utter depravity, the wrath of God and the proximity of hell. And they are not called to repentance because the Kingdom of Heaven is at hand but because their sepulchres lack whitewash and their phylacteries are not broad enough. If anyone thinks this is ancient history I need only refer to a recent correspondence on the subject in one of the British Catholic weeklies.

The fact that authority is vested in the bishops and clergy should not conceal the distortions perpetrated by those who obey, mostly laymen but also clergy as individuals under authority. Devious are the paths pursued by the consciences of people who congratulate themselves on the exercise of a proper Christian freedom when all they have done is to develop a double standard of morality.[1] They conform to the exterior forms of Catholicism and remain safely within the fold, but their obedience is not the response of love but only a self-justificatory surface to disguise (from themselves as well as from others) the fact that their hearts do not belong to Christ in his Church but only to themselves. Doubt of the Church's teaching is not in itself ignoble. A bitter struggle to reach a reinterpretation of some aspect of it whose present form appears inconsistent with the truth of her nature is perfectly compatible with a passionate love for

[1] Rahner, 'Mute heresy,' *Nature and Grace.*

and obedience to the authority of Christ in her. Such a course may be painful and testing and can even lead to exclusion from the Church, in which case the under-cover rebel feels very smug. But the honest reformer builds up the Church, even when he appears to be in conflict with her, while the double-think Catholic betrays her from the inside.

Yet how much is he to blame when the only notion of obedience that he has acquired from a Catholic educa-tion is one of sheep-like submission to authority? The conviction that freedom of conscience is fundamental to human dignity is there to lend its powerful support to his pathetic attempt to reconcile wrongly understood free-dom with a political-type authority. It can't be done. So the conscience whose proper function is to be the launch-ing base for the soul's flight towards God becomes instead a cage decorated with *trompe l'oeil* vistas of illusory freedom.

No Catholic who is committed to the service of Christ in his Church can find it anything but horrible to have to testify openly to the existence of such sores on the body of the Bride of Christ. To be obliged to hurt some-one one loves is to feel the shame and pain in oneself. But to relax instead into a facile optimism is not a real service.

The future is full of hope, but only if the past and the present are fully understood. Even these few examples of the ravages caused by the loss of a true idea of Christian freedom should be enough to show that this matter is fundamental to the Church's renewal. The understand-ing and use of true freedom formed the Church, and the desire for it preserved her even in the days when it was least understood and least effective. In the end it was the means of her renewal. The false interpretation of freedom, and its consequent denigration in the Church, restricted her mission, retarded her development, and could still make her new impulse ineffective. The interior freedom of an honest conscience assisted by exterior freedom from fear is essential for growth to personal maturity, for without it the full response of love is impossible. This is true for the individual and it is true for the Church of Christ. 'For you did not receive a spirit of slavery to fall back into fear, but you have received the spirit of sonship. When we cry, "Abba! Father!" it is the Spirit himself bearing witness with our spirit that we are the children of God, and if children, then heirs, heirs of God and fellow-heirs with Christ, provided we suffer with him in order that we may also be glorified with him.'

Existential Reactions
Against Scholasticism

G. F. POLLARD

THE aim and object of this essay is a positive one; namely to endeavour to show forth 'all the treasures of wisdom and knowledge' which are contained within the Roman Catholic tradition. For it is this tradition which has given birth to so many saints and mystics, poets and prophets, who by their wisdom and insight have immeasurably enriched both the Church and the world. The fact that the Church can produce such outstanding men and women is a clear indication that, at the heart of this great organism and organization, there lies concealed a divine truth and dynamism capable of raising the spiritual consciousness of mankind, and thereby transforming human society.

But the non-Catholic reader may well ask: 'If, then, what you say is true, how is it that the Church apparently exerts so small an influence on the general state of the world today? Why is it that all men of good will, particularly the young and idealistic, not only fail to recognize this great dynamo of spiritual regeneration in their midst, but even, in many cases, desert the Faith in which they have been born and bred, once they are free of the leading reins imposed during school and childhood days?'

It is a legitimate question, and one that calls for an honest answer, even though it may not be to the liking of many good and well-intentioned people within the Church itself. One can only say that in some wholly unforeseen yet in some sense divinely ordained fashion, the great 'fountain of living water' which springs up in the heart of the Church 'unto life everlasting', has been covered over and concealed by an inadequate theory of knowledge and a naturalistic critique of revelation.

First, then, I shall endeavour to show how scholasticism has driven a wedge between reason and revelation, between nature and supernature, and between the sacred and the secular; and that this process has gone on for hundreds of years. Second, I shall try to indicate that the findings of modern psychology—particularly Jungian psychology and depth analysis, point the way back to healthful living in the Church; and that they bear out the deepest experiences of the mystics. Finally, by taking the example of some of the greatest Fathers and theologians of the early Church, I hope to demonstrate that scholasticism is a radical deviation from the normal Catholic tradition, in that it sunders the divine-human link in man, and places theology in a watertight compartment hermetically sealed off from the influences of the so-called secular sciences. By the same token it fails to exercise that dynamic and creative influence upon the social life of the modern world which the world rightly seeks and expects from a genuine Christian philosophy.

Summed up very shortly, it might be said that the scholastics regard knowledge as being the result of reasoning, instead of being—as Aristotle held—the outcome of our union with all being, finite and infinite. Man is equated with the conscious mind alone, without any subconscious—or at least any subconscious that can be known. The inevitable conclusion is that the higher knowledge which we call revelation is something gratuitously given from without from the God whom by nature we cannot know. Faith, from the scholastic point of view, consists in an intellectual assent to something which we know nothing whatever about. It is not without good reason that the theologians of the Eastern tradition consider that the Western tradition is essentially agnostic, since it limits cognition too much to the sensuous world, and that there is one uninterrupted line of agnostic philosophy from St Thomas Aquinas to Hegel (cf. *Soloviev*, E. Munzer). Thus reality is equated with the consciousness of the average man, and the higher consciousness of the mystic is regarded as being inexpressible, and therefore non-educative. But, as Tillich has said, there is such a thing as 'ecstatic reasoning', and it is precisely the fruits of this transcendental reasoning which the mystics are able to give us. Yet the scholastics, following St Thomas, specifically reject mystical 'illumination' in their theory of knowledge, thus depriving the Church of one of its richest sources of insight and inspiration. The way in which scholasticism has inadvertently cut off the fountain of life from its source, and thus impoverished the whole life of the Church, is nothing less than lamentable and intellectually shocking.

Fortunately there is a growing recognition, among

scholars, of the responsible part that the human psyche, both in its conscious and subconscious aspects, has always played, and must continue to play, in the mediation of revelation to mankind. That there truly is a 'wind of change' blowing throughout the Church on this vital topic was illustrated by the rejection of the scholastic schema on the 'Sources of Revelation' by the conciliar Fathers at the first session of the second Vatican Council. Along with this one feels that there is a growing realization that it is largely due to certain scholastic formulations that revelation, whether Primitive or Christian, tends to be conceived as something exclusively 'ab extra', descending, as it were, from the clouds of heaven. Until recently the assumption has been that God has no need of man's help as a conscious and willing medium of Revelation. Such an attitude most probably stems from the opinion of St Thomas Aquinas that prophets are to be regarded as purely passive like 'brute beasts' in relation to the inspirations of the Holy Spirit. They, he says, 'are rather acted upon than act.'[1]

Father Victor White, O.P., in chapter VII of his book, *God and the Unconscious*, collates a number of similar texts which he declares to be 'shocking . . . to sweet reasonableness', but which—as a committed Thomist—he attempts to explain away: quite unsatisfactorily in my opinion! Thus, far from revelation being the divine response to man's yearnings and aspirations and his heroic efforts to develop his spiritual consciousness, it may—says St Thomas—be clean contrary to the recipient's will.[2] The prophet's vision is something that is done to him and which seizes him and overpowers him compulsively.[3] Prophetic insight as

[1] 'Magis aguntur quam agunt': *De Ver.* XII, 3 ad 19.
[2] *De Ver.* XII, 12.   [3] *De Ver.* XII, 1; *Summa Theol.* I–II. 171–2, etc.

such is independent of good morals, let alone personal sanctity.[1] It is the melancholic man who is the best dreamer, irrespective of his morals.[2]

But are not all the mystics introverted intuitives at some stage of their spiritual development? The prophet is 'the mystic in action', and though—contrary to the mystics generally—his union with God is a functional one, his experience has none the less an essentially mystical character. Prophetic experience, says Harold Knight, is 'a variety of that immediate and experimental knowledge of God which is claimed by all the mystics.'[3] And so while the prophet and mystic undoubtedly possess—as Aquinas suggests—a certain natural insight, they cannot develop this natural aptitude, in such a way as to become teachers of men, without following a path of spiritual realization. 'One of the marks of the true mystic', says Leuba, 'is the tenacious and heroic energy with which he pursues a definite moral ideal.'[4] This experiential knowledge of God 'is arrived at by an arduous psychological and spiritual process—the so-called Mystic Way—entailing the complete remaking of character and the liberation of a new, or rather latent, form of consciousness; which imposes on the self the condition which is sometimes inaccurately called "ecstasy", but is better named the Unitive State.'[5] How different from this is Aquinas' conception, which does not hesitate to draw the parallel between the inspired prophet and the 'raging maniac' (*furiosus*), the man whose 'mind is possessed' (*mente captus*).'

This theory of unilateral relationship between God and man, whereby Revelation is considered to be one-sidedly divine rather than divine-human, was a

[1] *De Ver.* XII, 5; I–II, 172, 4.   [2] *De Div. per Somn.* 33ff.
[3] *The Hebrew Prophetic Consciousness.*
[4] Quoted by Evelyn Underhill, *Mysticism*, p. 91.
[5] *Op. cit.* p. 81.

complete departure from the patristic tradition, while at the same time it is contradicted by the findings of modern psychology and depth analysis; for both St John of the Cross and C. G. Jung tell us that the path of mystical unfoldment and the process of individuation (between which there is an extremely close connexion), demand an heroic effort on the part of him who is following the pilgrim path towards Self-realization. Without Self-realization there can be no divine Revelation, for Revelation is nothing more than the enunciation of Truth as seen by the illumined consciousness. The conclusion is inevitable that when St Thomas wrote these treatises he had not achieved that integral, intuitive insight which transcends the barrier set by rational, discursive knowledge between God and man, the natural and the supernatural, the finite and the infinite. It is of this intuitive knowledge that Ruysbroeck speaks when he says: 'What we are, that we behold, and what we behold, that we are. Our thought, our life and our being are uplifted in simplicity and are made one with truth.' It is precisely this knowledge which the prophets possess, and to say anything less is to reduce them to the status of the shaman and the spiritualistic medium.

The truth is that St Thomas was too deeply influenced by certain aspects of Greek philosophy which place an unsurmountable barrier between God and man. Aristotelianism was a very poor basis upon which to found a Christian philosophy, for—as the Abbé Bremond demonstrates in his book, *Prayer and Poetry*—Aristotle specifically set out to *depoetise* the poetical or intuitive talent (which is the natural basis of mysticism), and to exorcise it completely from his right little, tight little republic. He did not deny the possibility of mystical experience and insight, but considered it too high a goal to set the average man. Worst of all, he considered the prophet a positive menace to 'law and order' and so was determined to get rid of him. It was expedient that 'one man should die for the people', and that human freedom and personality should be sacrificed to society. How far has this attitude crept into the Church, in its purely human aspect? One thinks of the Roman dycasteries in general and the Holy Office in particular. For it is undeniable that Aquinas' view of the nature of revelation inevitably involves—though he was no doubt unaware of it—the denial of man's creative freedom. The formalist and intellectualist 'bloc' of Aristotelian teaching has profoundly and adversely influenced scholastic philosophy. A closed system of doctrine and morals must inevitably result from it.

Yet another pernicious result of such scholastic categories is the implicit assumption that man can learn nothing from the development of his own spiritual consciousness. The traditional view that the perfection of knowledge and the perfection of character go together remains unheeded. This means, in effect, that theology and mysticism are kept in two watertight compartments. At the same time a disastrous dichotomy is created between nature and supernature. God is thought of as a kind of intellectual elephantiasis—a colossal magnification and multiplication of the conscious, analytical mode of knowledge.

How different from this essentially naturalistic metaphysics is the true Christial ideal! When Our Lord calls us to 'repent' he is demanding of us an ascension to a higher mode of consciousness, which does not dispense with reason, but uses it as its instrument. The Greek word translated as 'repentance' is *'meta-noia'*. It is a change of consciousness which belongs, not to the natural man, but to the secret, internal, spiritual man. It is not merely penitence or regret, but a revolution in our outlook, a higher level of understanding, a replacement of ignorance or '*avidya*' by knowledge or '*vidya*'. It is a rebirth, another step in evolution. 'Unless a man be born anew he cannot see the Kingdom of God,' said Christ to Nicodemus; while St Peter admonished the Jews: 'Repent and be turned.'[1]

Again we are urged by the Lord to 'turn and become as little children' and to become responsive to the magic and mystery of the world. But in that objective scholastic philosophy of 'reason and common sense' we have become like squirrels in a revolving cage, and the mystery of life has been destroyed for us. It is for this reason that seminary theology is so lacking in creative thought. The living and existentially experienced God of Abraham, Isaac and Jacob has been reduced to abstract and lifeless concepts. For the 'almighty and everlasting God'—a phrase which so often occurs in our liturgy—is not absolute in the Aristotelian sense of 'pure act' and 'unmoved mover'. He is the God of the Bible, endowed with an active and dramatic inner life. He is not static. He can only be understood dynamically. To think of Him as 'unmoved mover' is to look at him from the purely rational point of view. He is not a *phenomenon* or object of abstract speculation, but a *noumenon* to be experienced by the transcendental man in the depths of his being. Thus the Palamite theologians of the Eastern Church hold that the Scholastic concept of 'pure act' cannot be reconciled with the operation of the Divine energies or '*energon*' in man's soul, and believe that while it is perfectly possible to reconcile Roman Catholicism and Palamism, it is 'impossible to insert and acclimatize the latter theology in the rigid forms of Thomism.'[2]

[1] Acts 3. 19.
[2] Cf. Fr. Cyprien Kern, quoted by G. Dejaifre in *Rediscovering Eastern Christendom*, p. 59.

It is sheer anthropomorphism to imply that God is unknown in the inner depths of the human psyche—that He exists only as a self-satisfied and self-sufficient autocratic potentate to hand down Revelation 'ab extra', independent of man's own striving and seeking, independent of the aspiring Eros (which Gregory of Nyssa describes as 'love strained to intensity') reaching up to embrace the descending Agape of divine love. To Him indeed all things are possible, but not by the arbitrary 'fiat' of His will or the exercise of authority. Man must respond to His expectations in love, freedom and creativity. Only thus can the divine designs be fulfilled. The God who, foreseeing all, nevertheless consented to create man and the world, and thus made himself responsible for suffering, evil and final damnation, is a sheer rationalization. It is this Aristotelian and Thomistic doctrine of causality, determinism and domination which logically results in the horrible concept of predestination, and the unresolvable antinomy between grace and free will. The concept of causality is something that belongs exclusively to the phenomenal world. In the noumenal world God does not cause anything. Grace must be considered not as causative determination acting from above, but rather as divine freedom acting within human freedom. 'Grace,' says Nicolas Berdyaev, 'is the eternal bond between the transcendent man and God.'

God's action in the noumenal world would be more properly described as creativity rather than causation. Man co-operates in this creativity in the divine-human encounter, and finds uninhibited freedom in the realization of his transcendent Self. Thus while motionlessness and eternal rest might well be ascribed to what Eckhart terms the 'Godhead'; the God revealed in Jesus Christ is involved in the suffering of His creatures and in the process of redemption wherein—as St Paul says—the whole cosmos 'groaneth and travaileth in pain' until all things are 'summed up in Christ'. 'The idea that God suffers in History', says Reinhold Niebuhr, 'is implicit in the whole Hebraic-prophetic idea that God is engaged and involved in history, and is not some "unmoved mover" dwelling in eternal equanimity.' It is the anthropomorphic parody of God which the atheists and humanists have rejected. It is not God they despise, but man's unworthy idea of Him. Such intellectual knowledge, without the heart-experience, amounts to nothing more than that 'avidya' or Ignorance which Jung has castigated as 'Sin with a capital "S" and Evil "par excellence".'

Revelation, then, must be considered as a continuing inward and spiritual event arising out of the divine-human exchange or dialogue. For to claim that the revelation of the truth which bestows freedom is final and incomplete is, as Berdyaev has said, 'to fall into the wiles of anti-Christ and the seductive snare of the Grand Inquisitor.'[1] Such a view of revelation inevitably results in the minimizing of the prophetic and charismatic spirit which is the Church's crowning glory, whereby she merits to be the true servant and Mother of mankind. For it is in her womb that the transcendent man is brought to birth. But when the patriarchal principle or paternal element of hierarchy and organization becomes unduly predominant, then authority tends to lose its pastoral character and become an instrument of suppression where man's creative freedom is concerned. This is the whole burden of the current complaints against the operations of the Holy Office and certain Roman dycasteries; and again and again the Fathers of the Vatican Council have, either implicitly or explicitly, pointed to

[1] Cf. *Truth and Revelation.*

scholastic categories of thought as being the prime source of such aberrations. This was particularly noticeable in the debates on the schemas concerning the Sources of Revelation and the Nature of the Church.

Thus formalism, apathy and spiritual inertia are further Dead-Sea fruits of an epistemology and critique of revelation wherein human insight is reprobated, and all our philosophy and theology is based upon agnosticism, bolstered up by fideism. As a result of the consequent dichotomy between human insight and revelation the idea is inevitably fostered that—relying on authority, written or established by long custom—one can travel the road to the Celestial City by just knowing the way. Thus the necessity of entering by the narrow gate and undergoing the experience of the Cross is not sufficiently realized. Learning the catechism and memorizing the text-books is simply not enough. It certainly does not provide that 'moral equivalent of war' which Dr Leslie Weatherhead has said to be the supreme necessity for the well-being of the youth of today. Nor can sermons in the same vein provide those waters of life for which people are thirsting. Intellectual understanding alone does not make the Christian. The concept can only be made real by going through the experience which leads to wholeness or 'holiness'; and to that integral, intuitive vision which is the traditional meaning of theology. For it is only by such vision that the '*conjunctio*' or integration of the head and the heart, the sacred and the secular, the natural and the supernatural can be achieved.

This insight, this state of psychological wholeness which is the perfect fruit of grace, is the absolute prerequisite of all Revelation, and its ultimate source. This was true of the Prophets and the Apostles and of Our Lord himself, whose supreme Revelation was mediated through his perfect humanity. Moreover without it the so-called Deposit of Faith cannot be assimilated by us as a living, existential experience, in all its 'heights and depths', as God meant us to possess it; and with all its capabilities of indefinite unfoldment. Until this intuitive approach is perfected and persistently followed, Christian unity will remain no more than an eschatological hope. It is perhaps for this reason that the Archbishop of Canterbury has suggested that it would be helpful if the Council were 'to develop more fully the value of Scripture and the Fathers as against the system of Scholastic theology.'

It need hardly be said that such criticism as appears here of the present scholastic set-up is meant to be essentially constructive and not destructive. It is simply in the nature of a small contribution towards the great efforts that are being made throughout the Church to reformulate our theological thinking in conformity with the intentions of Pope John in calling together the General Council. The majority of the conciliar Fathers have themselves expressed the wish for such a change; and so it can hardly be asserted that the teaching 'magisterium' of the Church—which abides essentially in the Pope and bishops and not in the Roman Curia—is still determined to uphold the outmoded formulations of the past.

The gnosis or insight which is so characteristic of the early Fathers—of Clement and Origen, Gregory of Nyssa and St Augustine—tends to be reprobated by the scholastics, as if there were something specifically theosophical or occult about it. This is because they attribute everything to grace and nothing to nature: grace being considered not—as in the Eastern Church with its far older traditions—as the seed of the subliminal kingdom of God which abides in every man by reason of the divine spirit breathed into him at the creation; but rather as a determining power from above sent down at the price of the blood-sacrifice of the Son of God. This horribly legalistic interpretation of the Atonement derives not from Christian insight but from Roman law. For St Gregory of Nyssa—as Père Daniélou tells us[1]— the Incarnation and the Atonement are virtually one and the same thing. Christ took upon himself our fallen human nature (the '*sarx*'), and 'redeemed' it by restoring to it the consciousness of its divine 'image and likeness' lost by the Fall. He did not do this in virtue of something 'supernatural' added to nature, but, as Gregory explicitly says, he made '*of our own nature*, in his body, the principle of resurrection.' It is a restoration of man to his *natural* androgynous state, the state in which he was created in God's concrete plane, 'with all those gifts which we now call supernatural.'[2]

Thus for Gregory the Atonement is literally 'at-one-ment'. It is the '*conjunctio*' of head and heart: the result of what we would call, in Jungian terms, the 'process of individuation.' It is that process of psychological and spiritual evolvement whereby the ego, split off from the subconscious, and hence 'fallen', surrenders its pretension to dominance, and learns to take its rightful place in the hierarchy of the psyche. Only then can Christ, the kingly Self, with whom we are intimately united in the depths, take his rightful place upon the throne of our hearts. Gregory speaks of his abandonment of the ego-consciousness as a mystic sacrifice which Jesus had already accomplished before he instituted the Eucharistic Supper: 'When he gave his disciples his body to eat and his blood to drink, his body was already immolated according to the will of him who by his power

[1] *Op. cit.* p. 16.   [2] *Op. cit.* p. 2.

accomplished this mystery *in an invisible and ineffable manner.*'[1]

This state of psychological completion which gives birth to '*sophia*', is termed by Gregory 'Wisdom's cup' and has a definite Eucharistic significance. He equates it with the eschatological meal—as Père Daniélou tells us—foretold in the Old Testament.[2] Thus it is a foreshadowing of that Eucharistic and ecumenical Church which will come to pass in the age of the Spirit. And so, in his commentary on the Canticle, Gregory indicates that the partaking of the mystic banquet is also a participation in the bread and wine of eternal wisdom, symbolized for ever in the Eucharistic rite where the risen Body of Christ becomes the source of life, making our own bodies and our whole being immortal. This is the essence of the Christian mysteries into which, as Gregory says, Jesus initiated the Apostles when he said: 'Eat and drink.'[3] It is, then, the Eucharist itself, the sacramental sign of the inner unity of God, man and the universe, which must be the basis of Christian philosophy.

Unhappily this insight into the 'mysteries of the Gospel' must ever remain closed to the scholastic mind with its fatal dichotomy between human insight and revelation. Thus Fr Victor White, O.P. was quite consistent with his scholastic principles when he declared that we 'cannot penetrate into the inmost mystery of the Eucharist.'[4] It is all part and parcel of the agnostic theory which makes an abstract epistemology, which sunders theology and anthropology, the basis of all our philosophy and theology. Tied as they are to the theory

[1] Quoted by Daniélou, *op. cit.* p. 21.
[2] Prov. 9, 5; Ps. 22, 5; Cant. of Cant. 5, 1.
[3] Comm. on Canticle, PG 44. 989C; *op. cit.* p. 21.
[4] *God the Unknown*, p. 13.

of a unilateral relationship between God and man, which overlooks the divine-human link inherent in every man, it is virtually impossible for scholasticism to achieve any deep and genuine insight into the mystery of the Eucharistic 'ecclesia' or 'koinonia'. Hence the impossibility of any valid and ecumenical scholastic theory as to the nature of the Church. Hence too the inevitable failure of the Theological Commission, deeply influenced by the Roman Universities, to produce a schema 'concerning the Church' capable of meeting the requirements of the majority of the conciliar Fathers. As Pope Paul has said, we must go back to our origins, and he symbolized this necessity by his pilgrimage to the Holy Land. For only in the mystical and existential theology of the early Church Fathers will we find the Christian unity which we seek.

It is beyond a doubt that St Thomas, in cutting off the conscious mind from the subconscious, departed from the normal Catholic tradition as expressed by St Clement of Alexandria, Origen, St Gregory of Nyssa and St Augustine. Gregory held that God cannot be known as a mere object of speculative interest, but only as an existential experience whereby he reveals himself in the depths of our being. 'The mind', he says, 'cannot place itself outside of . . . that Being who is above all beings.'[1] On the contrary, he tells us, it is only 'by a greater and more perfect concentration . . . that it (the soul) keeps on going deeper and deeper until, by the operation of the spirit, it penetrates the invisible and the incomprehensible, and it is there that it sees God.'[2] He is speaking in this passage of Moses, who by meditation and asceticism and a great effort of will inspired by love (that love which Gregory equates with the 'agape' of the Gospels), thus penetrated the darkness of the unconscious, the

[1] Op. cit. p. 41. [2] Op. cit. p. 29.

'covert which the Lord made His darkness round about Him.' Again he tells us that it is only by abandoning the 'association which the soul has with the senses', that Abraham was able to transcend his native Chaldean philosophy and so gain an intuitive knowledge of God. (What now of the scholastic dictum: 'nothing in the intellect which is not first in the senses'? It would seem that scholasticism has no more to offer than that 'native Chaldean philosophy' which Gregory explicitly repudiates as inadequate for the Christian quest.)

Only by rescinding from the distractions of the senses can 'reason receive the vision of God with pure and naked intuition.'[2] Thus Gregory holds that God can be known by reason, providing—as we should say today—that rationality is not equated with the conscious mind alone divorced from the subconscious. St Thomas, on the contrary, consistently holds that God is totally ('*omnino*') unknown to human reason.[2] This proposition was implicitly condemned by the first Vatican Council which declared that God is known by the natural light of human reason. Such is the outcome of a purely descriptive psychology which chooses to ignore the unconscious aspect of the human psyche! St Thomas derived this misconception in the first place from the Pseudo-Dionysius who declared that 'the God whom our reason reaches remains, so to speak, an unknown God.' He was also much influenced by the Spanish-Jewish philosopher, Maimonides, who held that it is impossible to arrive at the knowledge of God by metaphysics.

Again Gregory tells us that the Prophets, Evangelists and Apostles 'have become rivers for us, drawing their waters from dark, hidden and invisible treasuries.' This

[1] *Op. cit.* p. 38.
[2] Cf. *Quaes. Disp.* VII, 5 ad 14; *Summa Theol.* prologue, 1, 3; *Comm. on* De Trinitate *of Boethius*, 1, 2, ad 1.

wisdom, he says, springs from *ecstasy* (i.e. Tillich's 'ecstatic thinking', a change of rhythm, a higher mode of consciousness). Yet even Père Daniélou, obviously influenced by his Thomistic background, can tell us that 'ecstasy, being inexpressible, cannot serve the purposes of instruction.'[1] What a tragic contradiction to the explicit teaching of one of the greatest of the Fathers! It is this scholastic schizophrenia which is responsible for so much spiritual immaturity and spiritual inertia. Ultimately it leads to atheism and godlessness, for who will accept a God who is no more than the conclusion of a syllogism!

St Gregory—who sums up all that is best in post-Nicean thought—St Augustine, St Anselm, St Bonaventure and Duns Scotus all uphold the Platonic tradition in Christian thought. In other words they hold that knowledge is mediated through the *whole* man, head and heart, and not made up by the syllogistic reasoning of the conscious mind alone—as is St Thomas' way. Augustine held that three elements go to make up the human soul: memory (by which he meant the Platonic 'reminiscence' or Jungian subconscious), understanding (the conscious mind), and will (the act of prehension, of reaching out to God with all the powers of one's soul). Our present dry and dormant scholastic philosophy ignores both these elements—the subconscious and the will. Hence revelation is conceived as something static, incapable of development: something to be received 'ab extra' from the God 'out there'. No modification of the human psyche as such takes place; no process of growing illumination and individuation. It is the essentialist view as against the existentialist; the objectivization of truth irrespective of man's spiritual consciousness. The philosophy of St Thomas Aquinas shows such a high degree of

[1] *Op. cit.* p. 38.

objectivization that one must term it naturalistic. It is a critique of revelation from the point of view of the natural man rather than the transcendent man; and while one must admit that such a critique may carry some validity for those who are unable or unwilling to see further, nevertheless the ultimate outcome must be a gradual cooling down of the force and fire of the original prophetic experience, and the decline of theology into the frozen torpor of the schools.

It is true that revelation (considered as the inadequate formulation of the prophetic experience, and *'par excellence'* of the illumined consciousness of Our Lord himself), is received *in the first instance* by an act of faith. But Gregory of Nyssa regards this initial act of faith as only 'for beginners'. It is the 'way of light' which he considers as only the beginning of the Christian quest. This must be followed by a 'further journey', in which the Christian, by *'apathea'* (meditation and asceticism); *'epectasis'* (creative activity) and *'parrhêsia'* (a child-like faith in God), must commence the arduous ascent towards the Unitive Way. Thus when Gregory uses the term 'faith', it is always in the sense of this act of pre-hension whereby the soul, detaching herself from sense data, proceeds to scale the spiritual heights; ascending, to use his own phrase, 'from glory to glory'. It is in the process of this ascent that the divine-human exchange takes place, and revelation is imparted to the human mind.

St Thomas, on the other hand, has rejected intuition and illumination at the outset, and thus for him faith remains simply an intellectual assent to a proposition. There is no 'further journey' in the sense of a modification of the human psyche as such. Hence his theology remains ever on the level of 'the beginners'— as indeed he states at the commencement of the *Summa Theologica*—and offers nothing worthy of the noblest aspirations of the human heart. Contrast this plebeian and prosaic doctrine of Aquinas with the exalted vision of the ancient Fathers of the Church, and it will not be difficult to understand precisely what has happened to the original magic and mystery of the Gospel message.

It is no wonder that he misinterprets the message of the early Fathers, and attributes to them an absolute apophasis which is completely contrary to their ideals. But, of course, Aquinas never practised what he preached. He was a saint himself, and that is why it has been considered incredible that he should have embarked upon such an agnostic and even atheistic theory of knowledge. No discourtesy, therefore, is intended towards the saintly character of St Thomas when we criticize his intellectual system. Towards the end of his life, when he enjoyed, we are told, a direct experience of God, he declared that all he had written seemed to him 'as straw'; compared with what he had now seen, and what had been revealed to him. We may well believe that St Thomas literally meant what he said, for all along he had declared that God is totally unknown. Moreover he henceforth refused to write another word.

The Thomistic innovation was fiercely opposed and even condemned outright at the universities of Oxford and Paris. A long time elapsed before it was allowed to settle down. However we may see herein a providential design, for as Ann Sallis Eley has observed: 'it is doubtful whether a Platonic philosophy would have withstood the inroads of inductive science without there first being a full exploration of inductive principles. Only a complete knowledge of the implications of a false theory can lead to its final rejection.'[1]

In the light, then, of the patristic and Platonic tradition one feels one must decisively reject the usual

[1] *God's Own Image* (White Crescent Press, Luton), p. 12.

Thomistic and scholastic conception of the *mode* of God's revelation to His prophets. For revelation is not imposed upon the prophet irrespective of his will or even of his morals, but in response to the recipient's religious, devoted and self-denying effort. Only then does the divine ray descend and transmute his human nature in its depths. Revelation is always initially from on high, dropping down like the dew from heaven; but it must surge up again in the psychic depths—a veritable 'fountain of living water' for those will take the trouble to descend—like Aeneas—into the underworld of the unconscious in search of it. This reaching out, or pre-hension, is what Duns Scotus termed the *habit* of faith as distinct from the *act* of faith, and it is precisely this *habit* of faith which the early Fathers held to be so essential to the process of revelation. For revelation, according to the traditional teaching, is not distinct from knowledge, but only a clarification of the natural knowledge which we already possess. It is the fruit of that natural union between God and man which grace does not supplant but only perfects. In this union it is our nature that is the substantial thing: grace is only incidental. The mystical union is only the discovery of the natural union by the operation of that divine, creative freedom in man which is what we properly understand by grace.

Augustine held that philosophy and theology are one discipline—as did Vladimir Soloviev, who sums up the Eastern tradition, in our own time. For revelation is only a clarification (mediated through the subconscious and by the effort of the will—to which God makes his loving response) of that primary knowledge which results from our constitutional union with all being, finite and in-finite. There is no true philosophy which does not treat of the finite and infinite together. Hence it is incorrect to speak of philosophy as being the '*ancilla*' or handmaid of theology. It was Peter Damien, Bishop of Ravenna, who coined this phrase, fearful as he was of allowing any genuinely creative role to Christian philosophy. Theology is not something which can be kept in a watertight compartment, but can and must be explained in terms of the rest of our knowledge. Only in this way can theology and science—as also theology and mysticism—be reconciled in a higher synthesis. But it was just such a synthesis which St Thomas rendered impossible by his underlying supposition that it is impossible to assent to the same proposition by reason and faith together: *'impossibile est quod de eodem sit fides et scientia.'*[1] In his enthusiasm for the Pseudo-Dionysius—whom he mistakenly supposed to be one of the Apostolic Fathers —he had come to believe that 'far from having any intuition of God, the human mind has not even a proper concept of Him.'[2]

Such an extreme form of apophasis can only be justified if we are speaking of the understanding divorced from human nature as a whole, including the other powers of the soul—the subconscious and the will. Moreover if we know nothing about the nature of God, neither do we know anything about His existence, for in Him essence and existence are one. Thus the theoretical question as to the existence of God—as posed by St Thomas—must necessarily contain a logical fallacy in its formulation. For he is unconsciously presupposing as the data of his argument a more primordial knowledge which we all possess. Unfortunately this presupposition is also in the minds of his readers, so that his systematic denial of the natural union between God and ourselves passes unnoticed; as also does his fideistic method of introducing scriptural texts upon which to base his

[1] *Quaes. Disp.* 14, 9, ad *Res* and ad 6.
[2] Cf. Fr M. D'Arcy's *St Thomas Aquinas*, p. 168.

natural theology. For St Thomas has already in his mind the idea that by reason alone we can only arrive at a negative proposition about God—'to know that *someone* is approaching is not to say that Peter is approaching'— and that any positive knowledge of him can only be derived from Sacred Scripture. Yet Scripture always presupposes that positive knowledge of God which derives from our natural union with Him. To say that faith comes first and that all other knowledge is derived from it is fideistic. This fideistic principle lies at the very root of the *Summa Theologica*. Thus St Thomas tells us in Chapter II of the *Pars Prima* that 'the chief purpose of Sacred Doctrine is to explain the nature of God.' Conversely he tells us that we cannot know the Trinity *because it is revealed*. Yet if we know any God at all it can only be the triune God, and indeed the drama of the procession of the three divine Persons is re-enacted in our souls. There is, in fact, no doctrine of Christianity which is not dimly perceived in the racial consciousness. Christianity only brings us superlative knowledge of what we already know naturally.

St Thomas' method is a confusion between agnosticism and fideism. He would have been saved from all this if he had not overlooked one vital point in Aristotelian epistemology: namely that knowledge is not the result of speculation but of our constitutional union with all being, finite and infinite. 'What man ever used a syllogism', said Aristotle, 'who did not know all from first to last?' Aristotle repeatedly tells us that because the psyche can be formulated in rational terms, this does not mean that the psyche is a rational entity. And so although, for purposes of practical politics, Aristotle chose to rescind from the imaginative and contemplative aspects of the human psyche and to banish the poet from his 'Ideal Republic', this does not justify Aquinas in virtually identifying the soul—this time, it would seem, for purposes of *ecclesiastical* politics—with the rational mind alone. The fact that he was not unaware of that poetical, intuitive knowledge which he terms 'knowledge by connaturality' makes it all the more unfortunate that he should have played the Aristotelian game of depoetizing the poet and emasculating the mystic in the interests of his excessively juridical conception of the nature of the Church. For there is some reason to think that Aquinas saw Aristotelian naturalistic metaphysics as a handy weapon against Albigensian Gnosticism, and —given his Maimonitite bias—there is no reason why he should not have used it in good conscience. But in defeating the Albigensians he also threw out the baby with the bath-water; for if one renders a true Christian gnosis impossible, then one is committed once and for all to a closed system of doctrine and morals in which 'law and order' reign supreme.

Not only is St Thomas' theory of revelation vitiated by his rationalistic epistemology divorced from its roots in the subconscious, but his treatment of the Gifts of the Holy Ghost suffers from the same defect. Their efficacy is attributed to grace alone divorced from nature in its depths. His failure is one of synthesis in that he fails to bring the ideal fully into the realms of the real in the ultimate question of individuation. The same objection applies to his supernaturalist treatment of the Incarnation. Such a view is incapable of comprehending a union between the divine and the human in terms of the psychological process of individuation. Yet it is in this very sharing of the Cross which we must all bear and the task which we must all perform that Our Lord became '*par excellence*' our exemplar, our mediator and our redeemer. We cannot achieve an existential understanding of the Incarnation unless we too attain, in so far as in us lies, to a similar realization of man's eternal hypostatic union with God. This is the ultimate end and aim of the divine-human encounter. It is by this work or '*opus*' that we are able to restore within ourselves the original 'image and likeness of God', and thus complete the work of '*apokatastasis*' initiated by the Greek Fathers. Only in this way will the Divine Humanity come into its own and the realization of the Cosmic Christ be achieved.

What we need now is a new '*Summa Theologica*' or summary of theology, which will have a mystical and existential basis rather than a rationalist and essentialist one: a '*Summa*' which will achieve a true synthesis between the head and the heart. If this great task—begun by the Alexandrian Fathers—is once more taken up and set in motion by the second Vatican Council, then it will indeed have achieved the purpose for which Pope John intended it: namely, that it should be the 'harbinger of a *more sublime* knowledge, feeling and vision' of man's eternal destiny. For it is only in virtue of a transcendent synthesis between theology and anthropology—thus bringing to light the divine-human link which all men have in common—that humanity can find salvation in its present psychological crisis; and the Church can become that spiritual force in the world which she ought to be.

As J. M. MacQuarrie says in *The Honest to God Debate*,[1] p. 187: 'This religious question of God is not a theoretical one raised by the intellect alone, but a practical question posed by the whole being of man. . . . Perhaps the question of God can be raised in a purely theoretical way, but this would not be of any interest to theology, and perhaps it would not even be a meaningful question. The *religious* question of God has an *existential* structure.'

[1] S.C.M. Press.

Questions to the Vatican Council: Contraception and War

ARCHBISHOP T. D. ROBERTS, S.J.

THERE are two issues of overriding importance facing the world and the Church today, and these two issues are closely interrelated: they are, as we all know, the question of limiting the population and the question of banning nuclear war.

I

The issue which in recent months has evoked the greatest concern among all Catholics and provoked the loudest outcry from traditionalists is that of birth control. A large part of this outcry stemmed from some remarks of mine which appeared in an interview published in *Search*. In that interview I repeated what I have said in various places over a period of years, that I have not been persuaded by the 'natural-law' argument against contraception. It does not seem to me to be conclusive, and if

I were not a Catholic, I would probably be compelled on the grounds of reason alone to accept the position taken by the Lambeth Conference, namely that there are cases where conscientious reflection on the matter by husband and wife might lead to the conclusion that contraception was the only way to save, preserve and sanctify a given marriage. How one could deny that conclusion on purely rational grounds—and it is on rational grounds that Catholic theologians base their case against contraception—has never been clear to me.

The Catholic position is difficult to maintain precisely because it is based on natural law; but such a position in effect assumes that natural law can only be clearly known by Catholics, in which case it has very little to offer other Christians, and as a consequence its 'naturalness' is highly suspect. On the other hand, were the Catholic position based on the teaching of the Church only, then it would not be binding on non-Catholics. Yet it has been maintained by Catholic theologians that it is as immoral for an Indian peasant to practice contraception as for an educated Roman Catholic, and this because the act itself is 'unnatural'.

This is obviously a matter that has the weightiest political and ecumenical implications. Is the Church to say in effect to the government of India that it is engaged in the fostering of unnatural practices among its people? Similarly, in the context of the growing cordiality between the Catholic and the non-Catholic churches, is it not an affront to Protestants and others, almost all of whom accept the viewpoint of the Lambeth Conference (which declared that on the grounds of reason alone one cannot affirm contraception to be always intrinsically wrong), to be told that all faithful Roman Catholics must believe that on those same grounds of reason contraception is intrinsically wrong? Of course, the political or

ecumenical repercussions of the present Catholic
position are secondary to the basic problem, which is
simply to determine the truth of the matter.

Now, I would not hesitate to say before the assembled
Fathers of Vatican II as I have said before Catholic
theologians, doctors, and other specialists, that the
reasons thus far proffered in condemnation of contraception do not convince me. Integrity and truth require
that I should say this. Therefore, I can only fall back on
the Church's authority; but I do so while recognizing
that this reliance on authority by large groups of Roman
Catholics who cannot follow the natural law argument,
must strike any Protestant observer as a contradiction,
since it is precisely the Church's authority—so we are
given to understand—which maintains that this *is* a
question of natural law. We should not forget the
agonizing dilemma of conscience that faced English
Catholics when St Pius V, after glorifying the secular
power as of truly divine origin, deposed Queen Elizabeth
the First and released her subjects from all allegiance to
her. Is there not a similar danger today of enthroning
human reason in theory and deposing it in practice?
Certainly one would think that any argument based on
natural law would be as cogent to one group of theologians or Christians as to another.

Where authority is concerned and where the question
is not directly related to immutable dogmatic truths,
have we any absolute certainty that this present issue is
not liable to the same changes which occurred in the case
of usury? The attitude of any modern theologian to
lending money at interest is totally different from what it
was about 600 years ago. Not only have economists
taught us many things about money that were not then
realized, but it has become obvious that for the larger
good of the community the taking of interest is conducive

to commercial, industrial, and consequently social progress. Certainly the authoritative teaching four centuries ago concerning salvation outside the Church is as different as possible from the position of the Fathers of the second Vatican Council on this same question. And just as contemporary theological opinion gives an entirely different meaning to the word 'Church' from that which it had in the sixteenth century, so too it is not impossible that the classic concept of 'nature' and of what is true of the 'laws of nature' will be radically revised in the future. Similarly the statements on freedom of conscience which have been proposed for acceptance at Vatican II are difficult to reconcile with the statements of Pius IX on this same issue a century ago. The fact is that changes do take place in our understanding of history and in our understanding of ourselves, and that the Church which lives and reveals its message in history can only be true to its incarnational mission if it responds faithfully to these changes, to these graces of each present moment.

There is no need to catalogue all the obvious reversals of position that have marked the Church's path through history: they have related to evolution, scriptural interpretation, and the morality of slavery. But one of these reversals is particularly pertinent to this discussion because it concerns a subject which is still used by Catholic moralists to illustrate their doctrine on sexuality. The traditional teaching on lying, following Aristotle and St Augustine, was that any disaccord between speech and thought was immoral, precisely because the tongue was the organ given for the expression of truth. Saint Augustine used the example of a man chased by gangsters and who took refuge in another's house. One may hide him, but one may not, for instance, tell the gangsters that he has already left and that if they hurry they may catch him. Rather one must let him be killed and, if necessary, let oneself be killed as well, rather than tell a lie. This view, now completely discredited, was based on the abstract ground that every use of the tongue required complete harmony between thought and word.

But most Protestants would apply the same kind of arguments to the organ of sex which Catholics now apply to the organ of speech; namely, that St Augustine's narrow definition of what is natural and therefore allowable did not take into account the whole purpose of nature in endowing man with speech; similarly, Protestants would argue, the present Catholic view on sexuality is in an Augustinian stage, because it does not take into account the whole purpose of nature in giving man the power of sexual union. The whole purpose of human sexuality is not to produce as many children as possible; it is to produce as many children as can be brought up to lead a happy and fruitful life; and the whole purpose of marriage must then be seen in this light.

To take a concrete example, an Indian lives in a mud-hut with his wife and several children, too poor to be able to afford any light or recreation and forced to find the major release from the strain of an impoverished existence in the love of his wife. The Catholic missionary gives him the alternatives—complete abstention or the 'safe period'. The attendant at his village clinic will tell him that the government has spent huge sums for research on various rhythm methods only to be convinced that they are doubtfully safe, and certainly impracticable for India. So the doctor offers free sterilization with the reminder that another pregnancy will either leave his six children motherless, or if the mother and child survive, add another stomach to eight already swollen with hunger. Similarly, the Protestant missionary will tell him nature did not endow him with sexual organs only for the production of children, but also and independently for the expression of married love. The Protestant missionary will provide a contraceptive not as an ideal solution but as a lesser evil than sterilization or abortion, as a lesser evil than the starvation of his children, the death of his wife or the death of their marriage. All of this the Catholic must condemn as 'unnatural'.

This was the burden of those remarks of mine which provoked the English bishops to declare 'Contraception itself is not an open question for it is against the law of God.' Now it is not a pleasant thing for anyone to have said to him, as they said to me, that I am 'leading people astray', or that I am 'urging pagan solutions with no regard for the moral law.' What I am urging is that the Vatican Council re-examine this topic with a view to clarifying the relation of natural law to contraception, and with a view to removing the stigma which led one Protestant commentator to refer to the Roman Catholic Church as 'an infallible guide to muddle and misery'. It is necessary that the Church should offer convincing reasons for its position, as Ronald Fletcher declared, for it is precisely the Church that insists on reason as the basis of its condemnation of contraception. It does not do much good, as I have already suggested, to argue on the grounds of a natural law that only Catholics are able to recognize as natural: a natural law ought to be a law natural to every being endowed with human nature. For decades now Catholic jurists and moralists have been advocating a return to natural law principles as the antidote to logical positivism; certainly nothing can so set back this cause as for Catholic moralists to argue on the grounds of a natural law which cannot be logically demonstrated. As the Secretary of the Newman Association Legal Studies Group, M. H. Penty, wrote in *The Tablet*, May 16, 1964:

> As lawyers see it, the question is 'Is the natural law something that can be established to exist independently of revelation?' It would appear that an affirmative answer is a *sine qua non* if there is to be any hope of gaining acceptance for natural law in this country as a foundation for, and philosophy with which to test, positive law.

Clarification, then, is what I plead for. And it should go without saying that this clarification demands that the people most directly involved—married couples, psychologists, social workers, doctors, pastors, theologians—be consulted and *be allowed to speak freely*.

It is with a view to this essential clarification that I have drawn up a number of questions which I hope would be commented on and supplemented by others, and which ultimately would be discussed by the Council Fathers. The fundamental question I would ask, however differently it might in the end be worded, must include the following notes: *Is a non-Catholic at present living under the vow of virginity, and seeking to enter the Catholic Church and priesthood, to be refused admission because his informed conscience cannot accept the condemnation of contraception by natural law?*[1]

The second question I would like to set in the context of problems facing India, since it is here that the issue is of greatest urgency because of the present programme of the Indian government and the poverty and malnutrition rampant throughout that country. For India, the limitation of families is the most urgent of all its social problems, and it is a problem that cannot but stun the Western mind by its complexity and its tragic character.

[1] Free speech would reveal torments of conscience among Catholic priests and advisers.

A visitor, for example, to a cemetery in a place like Surat, famous in the annals of the East India Company, may read on old tombstones of many wives and husbands dying in their early years and having buried with them whole families of young children. Those tombstones tell the same stories as millions of others throughout the non-Western world where medical facilities and scientific campaigns against a host of contagious diseases have only recently been introduced. The sad paradox is that it is largely the devotion and medical skill of Christian missionaries that is responsible for the population explosion as we know it today.

Moreover the problem facing the Indian is immeasurably complicated because in no country is the sexual act more intimately bound up with religion. So fundamental is the religious concept of husband and wife as 'two in one flesh' that the orthodox tradition of Suttee required the widow to let herself be burned alive on her husband's funeral pyre. Both the East India Company and the British government found it difficult to outlaw the custom simply because it was based on the same instinctive religious drives which, for example, animated the pagan fertility cults, or which found expression in the spousal relationship between Yahweh and Israel in the Old Testament.

Because of this and other factors it is no exaggeration to say that the Hindu wife has little to live for if her husband denies her the expression of this unity of flesh and mind. The Indian government, indeed, has made serious efforts to teach and encourage periodic abstinence. Not surprisingly, these efforts have failed in the face of such obstacles as those I have already mentioned and of such others as illiteracy, variety of languages, shortage of doctors and nurses as well as of the measuring or counting devices needed to make rhythm practicable.

Notwithstanding all of this, it is the claim of the Indian government's social and scientific advisers that the majority of the people now want to co-operate. Sterilization, when possible temporary, and always voluntary, is offered to those who already have three children and for whom any more could be an insupportable burden. Generally speaking, the Protestant bodies, whether missionary or not, have agreed with this policy and are actively co-operating with it. The question, then, that an Indian Catholic might put to the Council is this: '*Since the doctor tells me that another pregnancy will leave my children motherless, is it a mortal sin for me to ask for temporary sterilization?*' This question might well be followed by another: '*How is it wrong for the state to grant me for the good of my family what, according to many Catholic theologians, the state could impose forcibly on me as a punishment if I committed a crime?*'

Since the Council is seeking to be truly ecumenical, not only in the sense of embracing the entire Roman Catholic world but also inasmuch as its work is envisaged as opening the doors to those of other faiths, then it is obvious that the Council must consider these questions which raise such obstacles to any kind of meaningful interfaith dialogue. Certainly most of the non-Catholic observers would put very high on their list of priorities frank exchange of views on this matter of contraception which so complicates and often embitters relations between Catholics and Protestants, especially in mixed marriages. It is an acknowledged fact that the number of mixed marriages is increasing due to the breakdown of regional and religious barriers within individual nations. Many Catholic girls, for example, might well wonder about their prospects for marriage in a pluralistic society when they are warned by ecclesiastical authorities not only against marriage with a non-Catholic but also against marriage with a Catholic who may not share the official position on contraception.

The Protestant or Orthodox theologian is free to inquire whether the first Vatican Council did not merely proclaim rather than define papal infallibility, and whether this definition, which is now being elaborated by the second Vatican Council, must include the notion of 'collegiality'. Certainly if there is one field where this concept seems essential, it is in a declaration on natural law applicable to the whole world and capable of embracing Western and non-Western attitudes and customs. And such a declaration would be the indispensable prelude to clearly marking out the frontiers between conscience and authority.

The philosopher dealing with the 'rights of conscience' will recall that St Thomas established the obligation of always following a judgement of conscience made in good faith. Conscience is binding always, whether correct or erroneous. The Hindu widow believing that suicide by burning is a conscientious duty was bound to follow her lights, because an erroneous conscience is binding in exactly the same way as a correct one, providing only that its mandates are certain. An erroneous conscience indicates God's will for the individual.

The 'rights of conscience' was the last subject to be proposed to us in the Council at the end of 1963. It is a matter of vital concern to millions of people that the proposal should be adequately discussed inside and outside the Council, and by all concerned.

Any discussion of the rights of conscience will inevitably lead to the question of conscientious objection to war and to the preparation for total war. It is to these two subjects that I now turn.

II

The first session of the Second Vatican Council has already recorded in the words of bishops from many countries the profound distress with which Catholics must view our neglect of the problems of poverty in our time.[1] There has, unfortunately, been very little reference to one of the greatest contributory factors in the spread of poverty—the wasting of resources in waging and preparing for war. It would make a long and distressing litany were we to quote the exhortations of bishops of many nations in the last 100 years urging their faithful to second the efforts of their own national leaders in wars always claimed at the time to be just.

For obvious reasons Hitler's wars present perhaps the clearest case in all history of unjust aggression. The overwhelming impression left upon me by a careful study of Professor Gordon Zahn's *German Catholics and Hitler's Wars* is not so much shock at finding Hitler echoed over the signatures of great Catholic names: it is much more the realization that nationalism, mass hysteria, and above all, fear, paralyze Christian judgement. It is, indeed, a valid criticism of modern Christianity that it has almost entirely ceased to be such a leaven of peace as the life of Christ would suggest.

The factual evidence seems overwhelming that German Catholics generally—bishops, clergy, people—supported the Hitler war effort. No one, perhaps, who has not lived under the Nazi regime has the right to condemn the German Church on this ground. But we have the right and the duty to examine our own consciences, especially in free countries where governments do not exact a blank cheque drawn on the bank of conscience.

The rights of conscience: could anyone imagine a

[1] This section was originally published in *Continuum*, July, 1963.

greater contrast between the treatment of this question in, say, the *Syllabus* of Pope Pius IX and the language of Pope John's encyclical acclaimed by 'Everyman' to whom it was addressed? Echoing the language used in the charter of the United Nations, Pope John tells us that any human society, well-ordered, must accept the fundamental principle that a free human being is endowed with intelligence and free will. 'By virtue of this, he has rights and duties of his own, flowing directly and simultaneously from his very nature, which are therefore universal, inviolable and inalienable.' It follows that, 'as authority is chiefly concerned with moral force, civil authority must appeal primarily to the conscience of individual citizens . . . to safeguard the inviolable rights of the human person and to facilitate the fulfilment of his duties should be the essential office of, every public authority. This means that, if any government does not acknowledge the rights of man, or violates them, it not only fails in its duty, *but its orders completely lack juridical force.*' (Italics mine.)

An encyclical so novel in being addressed to Everyman, in uttering the thoughts of the man in the street, in its readiness to shock—as unquestionably it does—many estimable Catholics, has of course a long preparation behind it.

Surprisingly, recent research establishes that 100 years ago a similar proposition was made to the First Vatican Council by David Urquhart, an English Protestant diplomat very influential at the Foreign Office. A century ahead of his time, he sketched what practically amounts to a blueprint of the United Nations. He deplored the deterioration in international relations due to immoral decisions taken by governments involving whole peoples uninformed of the horrors of war. Then he observed that the Roman Church, about to assemble its bishops from all over the world, was the only supra-national body entitled and obliged to bring the world back to respect for fundamental human rights. He then requested the Pope to set up, before and outside of the Council, an 'Academy' which would brief the bishops on the technical aspects of international law, world order, world justice. Anyone interested in the details of David Urquhart's proposition may find it in *Collectio Lacensis*, document 364, page 1308 (text in French) where it actually formed part of the Agenda for the First Vatican Council.

It was the violent irruption of Piedmontese troops into Rome that frustrated this promising effort which could have been, if implemented, so fruitful for peace and Christian unity. It was a French priest who discovered the document only last year for the benefit of the French bishops who—almost alone of the national hierarchies— have been working along these lines for some time. They, perhaps more than any, have reason to congratulate themselves on the encyclical of the former papal nuncio in Paris.

The English Protestant effort of a century ago was taken up just four years ago by American Protestants. It was an inter-confessional gathering at **Spokane,** Washington, which invited me to share in its deliberations on peace when I was lecturing at Gonzaga University early in 1959. Pope John had just astonished the world with his proposal to hold a General Council. It was clear that the most practical co-operation we could give as Christians to his call for unity was to start intensive work in the field of peace and social justice where we have common ground.

My suggestion, therefore, was that we should petition the Pope to set up a *pre-conciliar* and *extra-conciliar* commission which would collate with the traditions of Christian morality the findings of experts in science, strategy, medicine, economics and international law. All of this was to be undertaken in conditions calculated to insulate the consultants from bad influences either nationalistic or economic. Some of the Spokane conference delegates suggested a formal petition which all could sign. In the event, they accepted my proposal that separate letters would cover a wider range of appeal, and escape the suspicion attached to anything remotely like a pressure group.

Many of these delegates told me that they had written to Rome, as many others have done since from five continents. Naturally, I have been asked by some of them why we have heard no more about it. I raised exactly that question at Rome in December, 1960, and discovered, when I had a private audience with the Holy Father, that he had never heard of the petition. The fact that he had not is part of a wider issue that can hardly fail to be discussed at the next session of the Vatican Council.

Both the theory and practice of Pope John underlined the necessity of dialogue between the Christian commissioned to announce the Incarnation and the Everyman on whom, in the words of St John, the Light ever shines. But there were, as far as I know, only three Catholics at the Accra Conference (Ghana) held in June last year. They were Archbishop Amissah of Cape Coast, Metropolitan of Ghana; Mr Sean MacBride, late Irish Minister for Foreign Affairs, and myself.

Mr MacBride and I had worked together for Amnesty International with the interests of which my own visit to Ghana was not unconnected, as we are both trustees of that organization. Mr MacBride also acted for Amnesty in Czechoslovakia for Archbishop Beran and others. The audience which I addressed in the Ghana Parliament House was, therefore, overwhelmingly non-

Catholic, even non-Christian. The very basis of the conference and its only hope of real usefulness was to provide a forum for free expression by delegates personally uncommitted to any of the cold war power blocs.

In this speech, I was concerned almost entirely with the declaration of human rights as set down by the United Nations. Article One I have already quoted as endorsed by *Pacem in terris*. Article Three says: 'Everyone has the right to life, liberty and security.' This point had been stressed by many Africans and Asians, who are very conscious of the threat to life in their involvement, with all the rest of the world, in a possible war destructive of the whole planet. Article Eighteen says: 'Everyone has the right to freedom of thought, conscience and religion.' In commenting upon this article I was, I confess, more conscious of the *Syllabus* of Pius IX than of the new tendencies, then not so clearly formulated as they have been since by Pope John.

My fundamental proposition was that we should ask for more specific concrete applications of the rights of conscience clause in the Declaration of Human Rights particularly as it relates to military service. Even 100 years ago David Urquhart's proposition to the First Vatican Council viewed with alarm the spread of conscription. Today that issue is, in most countries, a far more serious one than it was in his time. But because the role of conscience in determining our attitude to war goes far beyond the issue of direct military service, I preferred to use the term 'conscientious abstention' from all practicable co-operation in war.

It is in this sense that the Accra Assembly (which has now a permanent secretariat at the United Nations) asked for the recognition of conscientious abstention as a basic human right, and for the provision by governments of alternative forms of service. This resolution was discussed and passed together with a resolution proposed by Sir Robert Watson-Watt which suggested that an ethical code for the scientist be drawn up by the United Nations, with the hope that the code might become enforceable in a world court of justice.

In the two months' session of the Vatican Council last year,[1] any points I missed in the speeches (and let me confess that I found the Spanish pronunciation of Latin and the speed of Italian Latin serious obstacles) could be made up from reports by journalists in spite of their exclusion from the Council. In the four months which have elapsed since the first session, the secular press has informed me of much of what my brother bishops propose for the second session.

Since it seems to me ridiculous to conceal during the Council proposals which I have made publicly on four continents, I would like to discuss here some of my own hopes for the second session.

What I would like to see the Council do is endorse such declarations as those the French hierarchy made in June 1950. I discovered during the Council that this declaration is very little known in other countries, as it is in fact ignored in French official policy. Notwithstanding, the French bishops said clearly and in detail what Pope John has repeated in his recent encyclical. They were, perhaps, more explicit in condemning 'the use of modern weapons which strike indiscriminately at soldiers and civilians, and which blindly spread death over areas daily growing wider and wider . . . for our part we condemn them with all our strength as we had no hesitation in condemning the mass bombing during the last war which, in attacks on military objectives, killed old men, women and children at the same time.'

The fact that such a declaration by the French hier-

[1] i.e. 1962.

archy has proved almost completely ineffective throws light on what has already puzzled many people in the encyclical *Pacem in terris*. The best statement of the difficulty, and the best answer I have found to date, is that of Canon F. H. Drinkwater (his is a household name to all concerned with religious instruction), whose views I willingly make my own.

This viewpoint would maintain that while the advocates of controlled mutual disarmament are certainly entitled to quote Pope John's plea to the nations for reducing arms equally and simultaneously, and for the banning of nuclear weapons presumably in the same mutual fashion, the unilateralists are just as entitled to quote the Pope's words that mutual trust must replace equality of arms as a foundation for peace, and that 'it is hardly possible to imagine that in the atomic era war could be used as an instrument of justice.' The last quotation can only mean that atomic warfare is not morally lawful.

The solution of the seeming discrepancy is that in the latter place the Pope is pointing out to everybody the inescapable moral imperative, and in the former he is making an appeal to rulers on their own level of practical politics, and of what they are likely to listen to. This still leaves the unilateralists in the right on the main issue of morality. As to the forecasts of disaster if the West, including the USA, adopted the unilateralist policy, they are open to the criticism that they simply leave out of account the existence of God.

In short, the encyclical is either the merest starry-eyed theorizing or else it is a realistic call for an up-to-date re-appraisal of the whole present situation of the human race and what to do about it. I am sure the latter view is the true one, and that Pope John's timing will, as usual, turn out to have been well-judged. At any rate we must hope so; it is hardly likely that mankind will get another chance. Or perhaps instead of mankind we should say 'the white races', the disappearance of which (according to one American strategist) would be the only certain result of a 'nuclear exchange'.

The bishops with whom I acted in the matter of conscientious abstention shared these views of Canon Drinkwater, but they also thought it likely that no attempt would be made by the Council to impose obligations for which the world is simply not ready. My hope is, therefore, that the Council will recognize and endorse the right of the individual to abstain from doing what, to him, is clearly wrong.

The commission of experts, which was to apply this principle to the doctrine of deterrence, and from which we had hoped for light from the moralist informed by the scientist, has not materialized. So far, we have no more than discussion on the moral issue of intending to do what we are forbidden. What seems to me preferable to conciliar or papal pronouncements on such controverted subjects would be the recognition by the Vatican Council, by the World Council of Churches, by the United Nations (in its declaration of human rights), that the individual has a legal right to freely follow his own conscience.

There had been little or no consideration given in practice to this matter until 1916 when England, introducing conscription, made explicit allowance for the rights of conscientious objection. The United States and other English-speaking nations have followed the British example—America half-heartedly. The fact that Catholic influences have nearly always been in favour of the kind of absolute obedience of which Germany under Hitler gives us the extreme example urgently needs examination. Professor Gordon Zahn has given irrefutable evidence of the length to which Catholic authority has gone in giving a blank cheque to the authors of an unjust war. It is tragic that essential human rights have been vindicated not by Catholic authority but by the secular judges of Nuremberg.

If then, the Vatican Council declines to endorse such declarations as those of the French bishops, the duty of informing the individual conscience becomes all the more urgent. Freedom to inquire and discuss must be granted to the individual. Whether it is or is not true that some recognition has been given to this principle of the rights of conscience behind the Iron Curtain, it is certainly true that some of the Western countries do have a lamentable record. France is a case in point, under de Gaulle. Italy is another, with a very recent example of a public prosecutor asking for a heavy sentence for an objector just because he *was* a Catholic and should, presumably, have known better.

No honest man can ponder the terrible story unfolded at Nuremberg without putting to himself questions about his own responsibility which he cannot escape. No religion allows evasion of unilateral responsibility in the soul's final judgement. The United Nations, registering the convictions of 100 nations, agreed for the first time in history on a charter of universal human rights. And as long ago as March 1948 the Peace Pledge Union was endeavouring to obtain the help of the British Government for securing in the covenant the recognition of the conscientious refusal of military service as a universal right.

Over the years there has been a steady growth in most countries of the recognition that a peaceful world demands a really serious approach to disarmament. The member states of the United Nations are committed by the Charter to settle international disputes by peaceful means and to refrain from the threat or use of force. The policy of all responsible governments is based upon an avowed desire to avoid war and to achieve total disarmament, since it is generally recognized that the result of modern war can only be completely disastrous. And this recognition of the meaning consequence of involvement in war has and also brought an increasing challenge to individuals.

Catholics, then, must break away from opposition or indifference to the United Nations. In our schools, universities and seminaries every possible effort must be made to implement the ideals sketched and urged by John XXIII. Catholics must follow intelligently the proceedings of the Vatican Council, and give practical effect to the late Pope's frequent reminders that it is everybody's Council. Catholics must imitate his readiness to co-operate with all their fellow men because they are actually or potentially God's children as we are.

Lastly, let us never forget, as we do all too easily, that there is a warfare which will never end on this side of the grave. That war with ourselves is part of our fight for peace. It is a fight where, as in all other fights, we must expect, with Christ, to get hurt.

THE AUTHORS

MICHAEL DE LA BEDOYERE, formerly Editor of the *Catholic Herald*, now edits the independent privately circulated newsletter, *Search*. *Search* has courageously published many thoughtful articles by different contributors on Christianity today. It was here that Archbishop Roberts, S.J., first made plain his feelings about the official Roman Catholic attitude on contraception, which provoked Archbishop Heenan's negative pronouncement in May, 1964, and the subsequent Vatican statements.

MAGDALEN GOFFIN, *Superstition and Credulity*, is the daughter of E. I. Watkin, one of the foremost Catholic historians and writers of this generation. A history scholar of St. Anne's College, Oxford, she is now married with two children.

JOHN M. TODD, *The Worldly Church*, a director of Darton, Longman & Todd, is the author of a number of books, a biography of Martin Luther being the most recent.

FRANK ROBERTS, *Authoritarianism, Conformity and Guilt*, is a Senior Lecturer in Education and Psychology at St. Mary's College, Strawberry Hill.

PROFESSOR H. P. R. FINBERG, *Censorship*, is Head of the Department of English Local History at the University of Leicester.

ROSEMARY HAUGHTON, *Freedom and the Individual*, is a journalist and the wife of a public schoolmaster.

G. F. POLLARD, *Existential Reactions against Scholasticism*, is a Catholic philosopher and essayist.

ARCHBISHOP THOMAS ROBERTS, *Contraception and War*, formerly Archbishop of Bombay, is a Jesuit and author of *Black Popes*.

SEARCH

Search Newsletter, founded by Michael de la Bedoyere, former editor of the *Catholic Herald*, was started in 1962. It is unique in the religious field in that it is truly a letter in which the Editor introduces and explains the whys and wherefores of each issue. 'Personal' is the first word in every issue. It could never have started but for Pope John's 'bringing up-to-date' of the Roman Catholic Church. It has, of course, many subscribers from other Communions.

Today there are very few countries where it is not read. A visitor to Moscow, after seeing the atheist museum, commented 'very tame compared with *Search*'!

Because *Search* is a newsletter, it accepts no advertisements. The space thus saved is devoted to one of its strongest features: 'Letters to *Search*'.

Search is published on the 15th of each month and is only obtainable by annual subscription, which can be started in any month, at thirty shillings from 59, West Cromwell Road, London, S.W.5, England, or four dollars fifty from P.O. Box 102, Garden City, Michigan, U.S.A. Postage included in both cases.

Companion to *Objections to Roman Catholicism*

OBJECTIONS TO CHRISTIAN BELIEF

Moral Objections: D. M. MacKinnon
Psychological Objections: H. A. Williams
Historical Objections: A. R. Vidler
Intellectual Objections: J. S. Bezzant

'Likely to remain a source book of the New Theology' is how *Twentieth Century* describes this book which contains the four lectures delivered in Cambridge under the auspices of the Faculty of Divinity. Published in April, 1963, it became an immediate best seller, and is now in its fifth impression.

THE BISHOP OF WOOLWICH: 'A book that leaves the effect of a moral and intellectual spring-clean . . . the work of Christians deliberately exposing themselves, because they love what they trust and trust what they love.'

PHILIP TOYNBEE, *The Observer*: 'A book which suggests a whole new area of discussion between Christians and non-believers . . . an extraordinary, thorough attack on large areas of what is normally considered to be Christian belief . . . Dr. Robinson would certainly agree that *Objections to Christian Belief* is a more deeply considered intellectual compilation than his own book (*Honest to God*) was ever meant to be.

'The aim of these Christian teachers is extraordinary enough—nothing less than to state as eloquently as they can the bulk of the modern case against Christian belief and practice. On the whole they do this with a vigour which might almost suggest flagellation, if it were not for the robust and healthy good sense of their general tone.'

Companion to *Objections to Roman Catholicism*

OBJECTIONS TO
HUMANISM

A Critique of Humanist Theology: Ronald Hepburn
Is Humanism Utopian?: Kingsley Martin
Is Rationalism Sterile?: Kathleen Nott
The Pointlessness of It All: H. J. Blackham

Edited with an Introductory Essay by H. J. BLACK-
HAM, *Humanism—the Subject of the Objections.*

PHILIP TOYNBEE, *The Observer*: 'Ought to be read by
all those who enjoyed its predecessor.'

A.R.V., *Theology*: 'These four essays not only throw a
good deal of light on what non-Christians intend
when they profess to be "Humanists" but also reveal
that some of them at least are keenly aware of the
intellectual objections to which their evaluation of
human life is exposed . . . It is clear, however, that
"Humanists" differ from one another as Christians do.
There is plenty of ground for fruitful conversation,
and many of the views that are eloquently expressed
in this book will be useful talking points.'

Church Times: 'In a way, the Humanists are braver
than we are. They hold on to their belief in humanity
and they selflessly serve it, while refusing all belief in
any life beyond this one . . . one may salute the austerely brave spirit behind such a book as this, and then
keep it as a very handy statement of what Humanism at its best believes about life and about men.'

NO NEW MORALITY

Christian Personal Values and Sexual Morality

DOUGLAS RHYMES, *Canon Librarian of Southwark Cathedral*

Methodist Recorder: '*Not a clerical lightweight attempt to be "with it" but a serious analysis of the foundations of Christian morality.*'

JOHN GRIGG, *The Sunday Times*: 'He is aware of genuine moral problems to which his opponents are blind, and he can very justly claim that he is trying to find a new basis for the old Christian decencies which rigid orthodoxy, without imagination or sympathy, could never hope to defend.'

SHERWIN BAILEY, *The Church of England Newspaper*: 'He rightly claims that an ethic of love, founded upon self-knowledge and a real identification with others, is more positive and constructive than a legalism expressed in rules, and his earnestness and concern must command our sympathy.'

The Catholic Herald: 'The Canon is entirely right to reject the external morality of convention and respectability, legalism of every sort; and he has some excellent psychological observations about self-acceptance, creative responsibility, and respect for other persons.'

Christian Action: 'This is not the revolutionary and shocking book that its detractors have led us to expect. But it is a generous, responsible and, for the most part, well-argued work which will help many people and should be widely read.'

Second large impression.

190

BEYOND ALL REASON
A Personal Experience of Madness
MORAG COATE

This book gives a first-hand description of insanity as experienced by a woman who had a number of severe mental illnesses and later made a full recovery. Those who are concerned with the treatment and care of the mentally sick will appreciate its special value to themselves. But the book has a much wider range than this, for the problems it raises take us to the furthest horizons of human experience.

Theologians, philosophers and many lay people will find much here to stimulate and challenge their own beliefs about reality and the nature and validity of religious and mystical experience.

'*A book of rare insight and almost incredible courage,*' J. B. PHILLIPS.

With an Introduction by DR R. D. LAING.

THE PILL
And Birth Regulation
Edited by LEO PYLE. Published by Darton, Longman & Todd

The Roman Catholic attitude to birth control has been the subject of a vigorous debate recently. In *Objections to Roman Catholicism* Archbishop Roberts, S.J. attacks the traditional teaching of the Church on the subject. Prior to the publication of this book, Archbishop Roberts had outlined the basis of his disagreement in Michael de la Bedoyere's newsletter *Search*.

The text of this interview is reprinted in *The Pill*, together with Archbishop Heenan's now famous statement refuting these views and Archbishop Roberts' reply to Dr Heenan in the *Evening Standard*, together with letters to the Press and articles from the Continent relating to the whole problem of birth control. *Paperback*.

291/